CHURCH IN HISTORY SERIES

THE CHURCH
OF THE RENAISSANCE
AND REFORMATION

Decline and Reform
from 1300
to 1600

BY
KARL H. DANNENFELDT

CONCORDIA PUBLISHING HOUSE

SAINT LOUIS ● LONDON

Concordia Publishing House, St. Louis, Missouri
Concordia Publishing House Ltd., London, E. C. 1
Copyright © 1970 Concordia Publishing House
Library of Congress Catalog Card No. 77-98300

MANUFACTURED IN THE UNITED STATES OF AMERICA

Dedicated to
the Reverend Paul L. Dannenfeldt,
my father

Acknowledgments

To Crowell-Collier & Macmillan, Inc., New York, for quotations from *The Harvard Classics,* ed. C. W. Eliot; to Princeton University Press, Princeton, for quotations from Desiderius Erasmus, *The Praise of Folly,* trans. Hoyt Hopewell Hudson; to Fortress Press, Philadelphia, for quotations from *Luther's Works,* Vol. 31, ed. Harold J. Grimm; to the Westminster Press, Philadelphia, for quotations from *The Library of Christian Classics,* Vols. XX—XXII, XXV, ed. John Baillie et al.; and to Roxburghe House, London, for quotations from *The Spiritual Exercises of Saint Ignatius of Loyola,* trans. W. H. Longridge.

CONTENTS

INTRODUCTION

This book is an introduction to the complex and often confusing life in the Christian church during the period 1300 to 1600. These three centuries witnessed dramatic and substantial changes within the Christian church, for these were the centuries of the Renaissance and Reformation. Here, told all too briefly, are the stories of the Babylonian Captivity, the Schism and the Conciliar Movement, the Renaissance papacy, the spirit of reform among the mystics and the humanists, and finally the Reformation in its various aspects.

It was an age of great personalities whose impact on history and institutions is still being felt. It was a time of courageous religious heroes, of sainted martyrs, and of great cultural and intellectual giants. It was the time when the Christian church began to be confronted by corrupting secularism, growing nationalism, and telling criticism. The attempt of the church to directly influence the whole life of society became untenable, and the clergy found their activities confined more and more to spiritual functions. The secular state and an urban culture, new developments of this age, had a profound impact in changing the medieval church.

It was a period during which the church experienced decline and then revitalization. The unity of the medieval church was shattered, but the diversity that arose did not mean disruption. The Christian church was reformed and strengthened by the struggle that went on among its members during these centuries that ushered in the modern world.

It is difficult for anyone today to comprehend how the

life of the late medieval Christian, lived in a world largely devoid of distracting and competing interests, was so completely influenced and governed by his religion. His daily activities and behavior, his visual arts and songs, his amusements and social life, and his entire reason for being, living, and dying revolved around the religious teachings of the Christian church which represented to him the divine order of things in a confusing world. The medieval Christian lived the whole year according to the church's calendar. He joyously celebrated the mysteries of nature and of human redemption together during the various seasons, as well as the innumerable saints' days that crowded the ecclesiastical calendar. As the situation demanded, he prayed to the patron saint of his occupation, town, illness, or hazard; but especially he fervently called upon Mary, the kind mother of God. While the line between right and wrong in his everyday code of ethics was primarily that drawn by the authoritative church, this was reinforced by established practice, common agreement, and the interpretation through reason of what was "natural."

The medieval Christian sinned, confessed, and in weakness sinned again; yet the hope of salvation was always there — a future blessed release from the trials and tribulations that were his lot on earth. Yet this very hope was fraught with fear and tension, for death would lead to a confrontation with Christ, who was often viewed as a stern judge who readily condemned despairing sinners to everlasting torments among the devils and flames of hell. The terrors of this evil abode were mitigated for the dying Christian by the teachings of the church which made possible an alternate fate in purgatory, where the punishment was severe yet temporal and where the time of suffering could be shortened by the prayers of friends still living and by endowed masses offered in his name.

That an all-pervading religious atmosphere was present and effective was in part due to the organization of the powerful medieval Christian church. From the small group of the original disciples, the followers of Christ had by the late medieval period grown into a vast "Christian body" *(corpus Christianum)*, an international community of the faithful to which almost everyone in Europe belonged. Basic to this unity was a complex hierarchy, rationally organized and modeled after the Roman imperial system, headed in the West by the pope in Rome. By accident of history and geography, the Roman successors of Peter had developed the claims of primacy, along with a firm tradition of orthodoxy, into a position of strength and leadership.

Assisting the pope was a varying number of cardinals organized into a "college." From their number the cardinals selected the next pope. In the secular hierarchy the archbishops came next. These administrative officials governed archdioceses made up of a number of bishoprics, that is, dioceses of varying size administered by bishops. The bishop had spiritual duties, like ordination and confirmation, and also exercised temporal management and supervision of the clergy and properties in his diocese. In each diocese it was the parish priests who performed the spiritual duties of saying or singing mass, administering most of the sacraments, visiting the sick and dying, burying the dead in consecrated ground, hearing the confessions of the penitent, and in general exercising the care of souls. All too frequently, like his parishioners, the parish priest was barely literate. He usually did not preach, at least not until the reforms in church life in the 15th century.

It was this secular and celibate hierarchy, centered on the pope at Rome, that provided the unity of doctrine, liturgy, language, law, education, and control that was so important in establishing and maintaining an international medieval civilization. Because of its influence and control, the church as an institution became synonymous with Christianity. Eternal salvation, the goal of every Christian, was obtainable only through the church, for it alone was the absolute custodian of the Scriptures, the creeds, and the sacraments.

The sacraments, the indispensable "channels of grace," were seven in number, that number having been established in the late 12th century but not made official until 1439. Covering the crucial stages of human life, the sacramental system led to an exaltation of the power of the clergy who held such exclusive and awesome control in their hands.

The sacrament prerequisite to all the others was *Baptism*. This rite washed away original sin and mystically united the baptized infant with Christ. This sacrament was normally administered by the parish priest, and the use of water was required. The sacrament of *confirmation* was administered by a bishop to children. Due to difficulties of travel and the slackness of some bishops, the sacrament was rather frequently bypassed. It was not a prerequisite for first Communion. Next in importance to Baptism was the sacrament of the *Eucharist,* or Holy Communion, the essential part of the Mass. The Mass, with its elaborate and complicated ceremonies, its costly vestments and vessels, varied with time and purpose, but all Masses were essentially the same — sacrificial rites in which the officiating priest (celebrant) mystically offered up Christ once again. By the late medieval period, the Mass had become primarily a spectacle, with much of the Latin liturgy being recited by the priest in an inaudible voice. The most dramatic and central moment of the service was the elevation of the host (sacramental bread) at the time of consecration. Originally the congregation had joined in the services by singing hymns, but this vocal participation had become restricted to choristers during the medieval period.

The Fourth Lateran Council (1215) approved the doctrine of *transubstantiation,* according to which the consecrated bread and wine of the Eucharist were miraculously changed by God through the power of the words of institution ("This is My body"), spoken by the officiating priest, into the body and blood of Christ. In the 13th century of Western Christendom, because of the fear of spilling the precious blood of Christ, the practice developed for the laity to receive only the unleavened bread, which, however, was taught to be actually the entire Christ, with body and blood. Although the sacrament of the Eucharist was the fruit of the Mass, the laity usually did not commune at Mass. Indeed, the average medieval Christian, afraid of being unworthy of Communion, communed very infrequently, generally only at Eastertime.

The fourth sacrament was that of *penance*, which consisted of three phases: contrition, confession and absolution, and satisfaction (penance). The sacrament of *ordination* was administered by a bishop, empowering a priest or deacon to fulfill certain spiritual tasks. A priest, once ordained, obtained an indelible spiritual character, or mark, and a power which never deteriorated or became inefficacious. The sacrament of *matrimony*, appropriately solemnized by the clergy, was in the West for the laity alone, since the Latin church regarded celibacy as a superior condition for its clergy. The final sacrament was *extreme unction,* in which the gravely ill Christian confessed to the priest and was anointed with consecrated oil.

Associated with the sacrament of penance was the indulgence. The origin of the use of indulgences was simple and harmless enough, as originally it was a remission of a part or all of the temporal punishment imposed by the church on a confessing sinner. During the Crusades a plenary, or full, indulgence was granted to those who died fighting the infidel—a good recruiting device. This was then extended to all who participated in a crusade and then to those who contributed a certain amount to send a soldier in their place. After the Crusades the use of indulgences was extended in various ways. While originally indulgences were granted for virtuous deeds, they soon were sold for money. Then agents spread the highly marketable wares throughout Europe. By drawing on the treasury of "surplus merits" accumulated by Christ and the saints, the popes could issue indulgence letters and release the purchaser from temporal punishment both on earth and in purgatory. In 1476 Sixtus IV promised the purchaser the immediate release from purgatory of someone already dead. Although this papal power was questioned by some and although canon law did not legalize such indulgences, the sale of indulgences among the simple people increased rapidly. Gone was the initial emphasis on contrition and confession; the monetary aspect of the traffic became uppermost.

Besides the "secular" clergy who played an active role in medieval society, there were the monastic or "regular" clergy (*regula,* "rule") and the lay brothers who, to a certain extent, withdrew from the world and the problems of life facing the average Christian. Originally the monks led ascetic lives of self-denial, rigorous discipline, and solitary contemplation. The vocation of a monk or nun came to be regarded by most men as a more perfect way of following Christ. The ascetic life was seen as the truly apostolic one. Most monastic orders were under direct supervision of the pope in Rome, where the generals of the orders also resided.

As the needs of medieval Christianity changed, monasticism of the old type was no longer of great use to society. To meet the changing needs, a new kind of brotherhood was brought into being; the friars ("brothers"), originally laymen, wandered about preaching and teaching, hearing confessions, and ministering to the poor, the sick, and the ignorant. Early in the 13th century, St. Francis of Assisi organized the Franciscan Brothers (Friars Minor or Grey Friars), the original mendicant, or begging, order. Another such order, the Dominican (Black Friars), was founded in the same period (1216).

All monks and their female counterparts, the nuns, took the oaths of poverty, chastity, and obedience. However, the orders usually became rich and powerful, and with wealth frequently came arrogance, sloth, immorality, general moral decline, and the loss of original ideals. This was especially so in the late medieval period as the monastic communities and the friars freed themselves from the supervision and discipline of the local bishops. Yet, it must be remembered that evil, as always, attracted the most attention and the good work done by the monks and nuns was often overlooked and unpraised.

The monasteries had figured very strongly in the intellectual life of the early Middle Ages, for the intellectual realm was especially dominated by Christian theology. However, in the monasteries of the 12th and later centuries the atmosphere was often such as to foster little advance in intellectual inquiry and study. It was rather the schools, usually associated with the urban cathedrals, that showed increased activity as centers of learning. From some of these schools there gradually developed the organizations of students and masters known as universities.

In the schools of the 13th century, philosophy, the "handmaiden" of Christian theology, developed into a system of inquiry called scholasticism. This was an attempt to use the deductive logic of Aristotelian philosophy to arrive by debate at new Christian insights and also to harmonize pagan philosophy with Christian revelation. It was Thomas Aquinas (1225–74) who especially developed the use of reason in support and in defense of the revealed truth.

Some of the scholastic reasoning bordered on heresy; indeed, intellectual and philosophical speculations in theology had always been a source of heterodoxy in Christianity. Others had been labeled heretics for criticizing the church's practices and clergy—which they had often done with good reason. The authoritarian church could not countenance the growth of opposition to its monopolistic dogmas and ecclesiastical practices. Obstinate individuals were excommunicated as dissenters and deviates. By the formula of excommunication, the unrepentant sinner was expelled from the church's communions, accursed of God and the saints, and assured of eternal damnation unless he repented and rendered satisfaction. Should a king or region resist the authority of the church or break its laws, the entire kingdom or area could be placed under a papal interdict until submission or correction was gained. An interdict (prohibition) meant the closing of the churches and the suspension of the usual rites and ceremonies, thus creating a dangerous situation that threatened the salvation of all in the area under the interdict.

The formulas of excommunication and the interdict were fearsome enough to hold most Christians in line, but frequently more drastic means were considered necessary. Obdurate heretics were burned at the stake as subversives whose presence in the Christian community could not be tolerated. As heresy increased in frequency and variety in the late Middle Ages, the aged Gregory IX (1227–41) introduced the Inquisition, a papal tribunal whose agents were directed to detect and try heretics by due process of law.

In addition to the charges made by heretics in the West, the claims of orthodoxy and papal primacy in Latin Christianity were challenged by the Eastern Orthodox churches. These ancient churches maintained that they continued the true tradition of the apostolic church with an older faith based on the doctrinal decisions of the early ecumenical councils. Because of regional, linguistic, and doctrinal cleavages, Eastern Christendom had broken into separate units: the large Greek patriarchate of Constantinople, which had included Russia, the Alexandrian (Egyptian) and Ethiopian Coptic church, the Jacobite church of Syria, the Armenian church, and the Nestorian church of Persia and Assyria.

There were many similarities between the Eastern and Western traditions of medieval Christianity. In both East and West, religion influenced every facet of life, and in both areas there was genuine piety, a strong tradition of charity, a passionate belief in miracles, and a willingness to make great sacrifices for the well-being of the church. Both had well-developed traditions of religious poetry and music, hagiography, religious drama and literature, and beautiful, costly ecclesiastical buildings. Both were active in missionary work among the surrounding pagans. Both had extensive systems of monasticism, with that of the East having originated first. Both existed in a feudal setting, and each held large concentrations of landed wealth. Both were heirs of the classical culture of Greece and Rome and the doctrinal traditions of the ancient church. Both had a rich tradition of ritual and the cult of the Virgin Mary and the saints.

There were differences too. In the West the early efforts of the popes in Rome toward jurisdictional supremacy and the universal use of Latin had achieved a unity that was unknown in the East, where there was a strong tradition of autonomous national churches, each using its own vernacular tongue in its liturgy and literature. In the East, parish priests were allowed to marry; only bishops, traditionally recruited from the ranks of monks, could not. In the West, *all* clergy were required to be celibate. The strong popes of Western medieval Christianity had claimed and sometimes exercised a political supremacy over the rulers of Europe, while in the East the Byzantine emperor, the representative of God on earth, controlled the election and deposition of the patriarch and was himself a very strong figure in church affairs. Thus the patriarch's power in the affairs of the secular state was much less than that of the pope in the West. Eastern Christianity tended to be less legal minded and more mystical and speculative than the rather down-to-earth Christianity of the Western tradition, and the status of the laymen was higher in the Orthodox East than in the more clericalized West.

CHAPTER 1

THE CHANGING SCENE: FEUDALISM AND THE PAPACY

At the end of the 13th century, Western Christendom stood on the threshold of a period of dramatic changes. The two institutions most important in late medieval civilization were about to be radically altered. These institutions were feudalism and the Christian church, both conservative yet creative forces that molded medieval man and society.

By 1300, alien elements, in the forms of money economy and town population, had entered into the feudal system. New forms of wealth, based on a revival of commerce that originated in the northern Italian cities, were disrupting the traditional political, economic, and social pattern of the medieval and primarily rural and agrarian economy. Towns, peopled by burghers becoming increasingly wealthy, were slowly achieving political independence from their feudal lords and were affecting an economic revolution. Feudal society was being transformed, with the urban centers exerting more and more influence beyond the city walls. The new forms of wealth in a money economy opened up great possibilities of taxation to the rulers of Europe, who were thus increasingly freed from the limitations imposed by a natural, or moneyless, economy with its barter and services. The monarchs of France and England led the way in exerting royal authority, royal law, and royal taxation — erecting nonfeudal systems more in line with the economic and social changes occurring in their realms.

The Christian church was very much involved in the medieval feudal system. Bishops and abbots, the heads of monasteries, were holders of fiefs and manors, and the church's economic structure was closely tied to that of feudalism. Anything that affected a change in this basic and traditional pattern of behavior was sure to cause a change in the church. While the practices and dogmas of medieval Christianity were not immediately altered by the economic and social changes, the growing secularism, especially that of the urban population, had a decidedly adverse effect on medieval asceticism, otherworldliness, and religiosity. The love of money pervaded both laity and clergy despite the church's attempts to limit profiteering with the theories of "no usury" and a "just price." The papal claim of international authority and control, dependent as it had been on the political weakness of the state due to feudal decentralization, was directly challenged both by the rising monarchs and by the influential towns and cities. In general, the church failed to maintain the loyalty and devotion of the upper and middle classes, who gradually turned to the state for leadership.

BABYLONIAN CAPTIVITY

Late in the 13th century a conflict arose between Pope Boniface VIII and Philip IV of France over taxation of the French clergy by the king. In 1302 a council in Rome issued the historical bull called *Unam sanctam*. In firm language this bull spoke of the "one holy Catholic and also apostolic Church" outside of which there was "neither salvation nor remission of sins" and which held both the spiritual and temporal swords. In consequence of this power, Boniface. audaciously asserted that "it is entirely necessary for salvation that all human creation be subject to the pope of Rome."

William of Nogaret, an agent of Philip, responded to his king's demand for Boniface's deposition by briefly holding the pontiff a prisoner in his own palace at Anagni. The aged and humiliated pope died a month later (Oct. 12, 1303). After the brief rule of Pope Benedict XI, the archbishop of Bordeaux, France, was elected through French influence as Pope Clement V. In 1309 the new and weak-willed pope transferred his seat from troubled Rome to Avignon, a city on the Rhone River and just outside the boundary of France. Here the papacy was to remain for

68 years, the period of the "Babylonian Captivity," as Petrarch named it. Nationalism and the strong secular state had triumphed over the internationalism of the popes, who were never again to be in a position to assert exorbitant claims in the political arena. Indeed, the first decade of the 14th century is a turning point in the history of the Christian church and especially of the papacy.

It was natural that during the Babylonian Captivity the states of Europe outside of France would regard the series of French pontiffs as but "captives" and puppets of the French monarchs. As a result, in addition to the loss of international prestige, the popes at Avignon experienced declining revenues and reverence. Placed on their mettle, they developed a centralized bureaucratic system that was as efficient as it was often corrupt and mercenary. Coined money was becoming increasingly available in Europe, and papal revenues were greatly expanded by a variety of devices that often reflected unfavorably on the ethical standards of the papacy and its administrative and fiscal officers. Every possible source of revenue was developed. The immense, fortified palace of the popes which arose in Avignon was surrounded by the many buildings, great and small, that housed the growing number of officials, servants, and hangers-on. Although many of the popes and prelates of this period tried to live exemplary Christian lives themselves, the secular magnificence and the corruption of the papal court at Avignon tended to cause men to separate true Christianity from the traditional and international church and to think in terms of a national or even of a local church. This tendency was to become part of the Reformation movement in the 16th century.

The worldliness that characterized the papacy during the Babylonian Captivity was a part, on an exaggerated scale, of the general secularism that was spreading throughout Christian Europe in the 14th century. The growing pursuit of wealth and comforts distracted men from the contemplative life and piety that had pervaded much of medieval civilization. This secularism proved much more attractive than otherworldliness with its discomforts, asceticism, and prayers. Heaven could wait. Among the general laity, a relaxation in the efforts to achieve Christian ideals accompanied the growing disrespect for the clergy and dogmas of the church.

THE GREAT SCHISM

For almost 70 years the papacy resided at Avignon. Then, late in 1377, the invalid Pope Gregory XI and his reluctant court entered Rome, where the pope died the next spring. The new pope, Urban VI, launched an attempt at reform, striking especially at the sources of wealth by which the greedy and mercenary cardinals lived so luxuriously. Thereupon, the cardinals gathered at Anagni and declared the election of Urban invalid and elected another pope, Clement VII. Clement went back to the papal palace at Avignon. There were now two popes, one in Rome and one at Avignon, each with his own college of cardinals. The Great Schism had begun.

Unparalleled confusion spread through Christian Europe as each pope excommunicated the other and as the rulers of the West chose one or the other of the two popes as the true pontiff. The choice followed political and national lines and split Europe into two camps. Although Urban died in 1389 and Clement in 1394, the strife continued, for successors were elected for each. With each party declaring the sacraments given by the clergy of the opposite group to be invalid, the resulting confusion, doubts, and fears made many a pious Christian uncertain of his own salvation. In the widespread confusion, there were frequent appeals to a general council to settle the schism and to promulgate reforms in the church. In the discussion the University of Paris led the way.

THE CONCILIAR MOVEMENT

In 1409, in response to the urgings of many, a general council met at Pisa. When the council deposed the two reigning popes and elected its own, there were really three popes, since the two deposed popes refused to recognize the authority of the council. In 1414 a new council opened at Constance. This council asserted its superiority over the papacy in a revolutionary decree and deposed two of the popes and secured the abdication of the third. The Great Schism of the church was at an end after 39 years of confusion and loss of respect for the papacy. The council also issued a call for more frequent councils and elected a new pope, Martin V. Later, ineffective councils were held at Pavia (1423) and at Basel (1431). The council that met at Ferrara in 1437 was moved two years later to Florence, where an unsuccessful attempt was made to bring about a reunion with the Greek Orthodox Church.

PAPAL SUPREMACY REASSERTED

With the conciliarist movement at an end and largely discredited, the popes were able to reassert their supremacy. But it was a hollow victory. Involved in a bitter internal struggle for supremacy, neither the councils nor the popes introduced a viable program of reform, thus making the more radical Reformation of the 16th century inevitable. The entire period of the Babylonian Captivity, Schism, and Conciliarism had coincided with and contributed to the rise of secular authorities with whom the popes now had to share political power, leadership, and prestige.

THE RENAISSANCE PAPACY

The Italy in which the papacy once again resided was far different from that of the preceding century, for by now the Renaissance had come to Italy. The material wealth of the 14th century had prepared the way for secularism and for the enjoyment and support of the art, music, and literature that reflected that secularism. Gone was the medieval ideal of asceticism and otherworldliness. The dead but seemingly similar civilizations of classical Greece and Rome were taken as models for the new way of life and for the arts. The scholars who rediscovered the classical civilizations were called "humanists," for they were very much interested in the *studia humanitatis*, "the humanities," with a new emphasis on man, his deeds, thought, and dignity.

They sought to disseminate the classical Greek and Latin literature in the original languages, as well as the philosophy of Plato and others, in competition with the Aristotelianism of medieval scholasticism which they deprecated. Wealthy patrons, many of whom were upstarts of a new nobility, surrounded themselves with artists, with humanists and other scholars, and collected manuscripts, ancient coins, and art. Yet the brilliant, inspired artistry and the devoted scholarship were in marked contrast to the violence, superstitions, poverty, ignorance, and moral relaxation of the age.

The papacy and the rest of the ecclesiastical hierarchy in Italy became willing captives of the Renaissance spirit. The Renaissance papacy was often characterized by a secularism that made it difficult to distinguish the rulers of the papal states in central Italy from the rulers of other states. Thus Nicholas V, elected pope after a scholarly career, sought to be a typical Renaissance prince. He used the revenues received from countless Christian pilgrims to purchase the manuscripts that formed the nucleus of the now famous Vatican Library. His circle of humanists enhanced the papal court, while his support of architects and artists led to the beautification of a drab and dirty Rome. By these devices, instead of an intensified piety, he sought to restore the prestige the papacy had lost during the preceding century and a half.

The Renaissance popes that followed Nicholas continued in the pattern he had established. All were patrons of scholars and artists, and Rome was beautified with numerous new churches, chapels, and other structures. With the Renaissance papacy came flagrant nepotism, whereby the popes gave lucrative church offices to nephews and other relatives, who were frequently all too unworthy. An additional evil was frequently practiced. This was simony, or the sale of ecclesiastical offices, often to the highest bidder. The careers of the popes who reigned during the quarter-century that preceded the Lutheran Reformation are illustrative of the worst of the Renaissance popes.

Christopher Columbus had been at sea only a week on his epoch-making voyage when the cardinals elected Rodrigo Borgia, an energetic Spanish cardinal, who assumed as pope the name Alexander VI (1492–1503). In his reign the Renaissance papacy reached its lowest point in morals. A nephew of Pope Calixtus III, Rodrigo had been made a cardinal at the age of 24 or 25. A number of children were born to the cardinal before he became pope; two of them were the famous or infamous Cesare, made a cardinal at 18, and the devoted Lucrezia. Christian Europe was shocked at the scandalous tales, often exaggerated, that came from Rome. Alexander died on Aug. 18, 1503, unmourned, probably from malaria. Cesare was also ill at the time and was thus unable to establish the hereditary papacy he had planned.

Pope Julius II (1503–13) is remembered not for his piety or spiritual leadership, but rather for his successful military campaigns against his Christian neighbors. Despite his advanced age, the energetic and hard-swearing pope often led papal troops himself. His use of excommunication for political and military reasons made a mockery of this spiritual weapon. A great patron of the arts, Julius employed such outstanding artists as Bramante, Michelangelo, and Raphael to enhance Rome with beautiful buildings, sculpture, and paintings. The ancient and venerable St. Peter's Basilica was demolished in 1505, and an imposing, huge cathedral, the present basilica, was begun in 1506.

The fighting Julius was succeeded by the scholarly, easy-going, wealthy, and gay Leo X (1513–21). Created a cardinal at 14, he was only 37 when he was elected pope. His early papal edicts calling for reform were ineffective because of the opposition of those whose income would have been curtailed. Leo was noted for his patronage of artists, musicians, and scholars; the gaiety of his court; and his generous gifts. He pushed the construction of the new St. Peter's under the direction of Bramante, Raphael, and Peruzzi. How this building enters into the beginning of the Reformation will be seen later. His exactions from European Christians increased the number of warnings and complaints from those desirous of reform. But these were all unheeded in the happy center of Christendom that Rome had become. Leo, bankrupt, died late in 1521, unaware of the meaning of the revolt in Germany that Luther had begun four years earlier.

CHAPTER **2** •

ANTICLERICALISM AND
THE NEW SPIRIT OF REFORM

The secularized Renaissance papacy had lost touch with popular piety and with Christian ideals. The ecclesiastical hierarchy, reflecting the worldliness of the times only too well, was frequently mercenary, covetous of wealth, and immoral. To be sure, the officials of civil governments of the time exhibited the same sins and weaknesses of mankind, but Christians have always demanded and hoped for a higher morality among those who represented the church. It was natural, therefore, that complaints and demands for reform were common among Christians everywhere.

All the denunciations and complaints occasioned by the varied abuses, corruption, wealth, and immorality among the clergy, as well as their commanding secular power and offices, are summed up by the word *anticlericalism*. With the rise of national states and strong monarchs, anticlericalism was often motivated by feelings of nationalism and resentment at the great tax-free wealth of the church, the loss of money to Rome, and papal interference in the politics and economy of the national state. With the increase of a humanistically educated laity, frequent attacks were made on the ignorance of the clergy. Humanists from Italy and later from northern Europe called for a reform from within the church and used their training and knowledge to pen bitter satires and other works of condemnation. Preachers of reform thundered dire warnings from their pulpits, and everywhere shocked Christians prayed for reform and sought to live pious lives despite the poor example of the clergy.

JOHN WYCLIFFE

More subversive and more direct than previous attacks were the anticlerical and theological arguments pronounced by John Wycliffe. This English reformer was born about 1320 and became a renowned professor of theology at Oxford. With the papacy residing at Avignon and under French influence, anticlericalism ran strong in 14th-century England. In this atmosphere Wycliffe wrote English and Latin tracts and treatises containing statements and views on the church that clearly foreshadow some of the expressions of later Protestant reformers. He advocated that the hierarchy, from pope to priest, be judged by the most rigid Biblical standards. Since the secularized clergy were faithless stewards, they should be deprived of their power and property by the lay authorities, to whom God had given dominion over temporal matters. The church had been given dominion only in spiritual matters, and a corrupt clergy loses claim even to this. Like Luther later, Wycliffe undermined the spiritual power and authority of the priesthood. He also recommended marriage of the clergy. He denied the theory of transubstantiation in the Eucharist, considered auricular confession unnecessary, rejected indulgences, and exalted the Bible, "the law of God," as the infallible and final authority in the church. He recommended the formation of an English church independent of the pope, whom he repeatedly called "the Antichrist." With the help of two assistants, Wycliffe translated the Scriptures into English. Although he was condemned by the pope for his views, the protection afforded by the powerful son of King Edward III, John of Gaunt, enabled Wycliffe to escape death at the stake. He died a natural death late in 1384. His teachings, however, continued to be spread among the people through the Lollards, or "poor priests."

JOHN HUS

Bohemian students at Oxford took Wycliffe's writings home with them to Prague, where they found ready acceptance. The soil had been prepared by the reform preachers and the literature of the Bohemian *devotio moderna* ("new devotion"), a reform movement that emphasized frequent Communion and a thoroughgoing moral reform among Christians. The reform movement thus begun found a new leader in John Hus of the University of Prague, who was deeply influenced by Wycliffe's works. He did not accept Wycliffe's denial of traditional doctrine but denounced the traffic in indulgences, image worship, immorality among the hierarchy, simony, greed, and impious popes whom he considered antichrists. Despite opposition, excommunication, and a summons to Rome, Hus continued as an enormously popular preacher and writer. Under safe-conduct from the Emperor Sigismund, Hus dared to appear before the Council of Constance. There he was falsely accused of heresy, imprisoned, condemned, and finally burned at the stake on July 6, 1415.

The death of the martyred Hus created a national revolt in Bohemia. Under the formulation called the Four Articles of Prague (1420), the Hussites demanded the giving of both bread and wine to laymen, or Communion "in both kinds"; the punishment of simony; the liberty to preach God's Word without ecclesiastical hindrance; and the end of the wealth and secular power of the clergy. The chalice became the symbol of Hussitism, and the moderate Hussites became known as Utraquists (both kinds). Most of the Utraquists, however, ultimately became Lutherans, and Luther liked to call himself a Hussite. The more radical Hussites, the Taborites, insisted on even more thoroughgoing reforms of ecclesiastical practices on the basis of the Bible, "the law of God." They practiced a type of Christian and democratic communism.

SAVONAROLA

In Italy the voice of warning and condemnation was that of a Florentine Dominican, Girolamo Savonarola (1452–98). This eloquent preacher chilled vast audiences with his impassioned denunciations of the external abuses of his time. The corruption and immorality of the clergy and the papacy, the luxury and greed of the citizens, and the tyranny of the Medici were all denounced in inflammatory sermons by this precursor of the Reformation. Like the Old Testament prophets, he foretold the ruin of sinful Italy and the invasion of the French armies as God's avengers. When the Medici were driven from Florence (1494), Savonarola governed the republic that was proclaimed. The dissolute pope, Alexander VI, summoned him to Rome and ordered him to stop preaching. Neither of these orders was obeyed, and the friar continued his uncompromising attacks on the corruption exhibited by the pope and clergy. Finally, seized by his enemies, Savonarola and two of his followers were tortured, condemned as heretics and false prophets, hanged, and burned (May 23, 1498). When this spirited insurrectionist died, Luther was 14 years old.

MYSTICISM

The new spirit of reform was very evident in the work of the mystics who stirred the Christians of northern and central Europe with their widespread preaching and voluminous devotional literature. These mystics of the 14th and later centuries emphasized personal piety and direct access to God. They thus created a religious climate that was to favor the later Protestant Reformers. The mystics stressed the emotional religious experience, rather than the intellectual, and a life in imitation of Christ. They preached and wrote in the vernacular and thus influenced multitudes of Christians who longed for a simple religion along apostolic ideals. Their teachings centered on the *devotio moderna,* or "new devotion."

The *devotio moderna* received its greatest and finest expression in the *Imitation of Christ,* a work most probably written by Thomas a Kempis (d. 1471). As a devotional booklet, it stressed humility, passiveness, and contemplation while showing little concern for the systematic theology of the church. Strongly èthical and moral in tone, the *Imitation* was a manual for the truly Christian life (see Appendix, No. 1). It sought to prepare the reader's soul for the purity necessary for union with God. The reading and study of Scriptures was enjoined as essential for the preparation of the inner spirit.

CHRISTIAN HUMANISM

While the mystics sought an emotional religious experience, the Christian humanists used a more intellectual approach in expressing their new spirit of reform. With but few exceptions, Italian humanists did not concern themselves greatly with the Gospel. However, when humanism spread to the areas north of the Alps in the late 15th century, a Christian and reformist concern became more evident. Turning away from scholasticism, these humanists sought the true meaning of the sources of Christianity. Many of the northern humanists made excellent use of their knowledge of history and of Greek, Latin, and Hebrew to make the texts of the Bible and the church fathers clearer. In the light of a better philological understanding of the actual words used in the early Christian literature, new interpretations of the texts were made. This Christian humanism, as it has been called, sought to bring about a moral and educational reform from within the church.

Desiderius Erasmus of Rotterdam (1469–1536) was the most significant Christian humanist. Through brilliant satire and ridicule this international scholar hoped to affect a change in the ignorance, greed, and immorality of the clergy and the laity. In his popular *Praise of Folly* (1511; see Appendix, No. 2), he castigated the follies and stupid activities of mankind, but the clergy especially were held up to ridicule. Numerous and learned as his writings were, Erasmus' greatest scholarly achievement lay in his editing of early Christian texts. In 1502 he edited and published the first edition of Lorenzo Valla's critical revision of the Latin text of the New Testament. In 1516 he published his own very influential Greek and Latin edition of the New Testament, which bore ample evidence of his humanistic training. He expressed the hope that the Scriptures would be translated into all languages so that everyone would know the sacred words firsthand. In 1516 also appeared his critical edition of Jerome. This was followed later by editions of Augustine, Basil, Ambrose, and other early church writers. All these texts were to be used by the Reformers. It is no wonder that even in his lifetime Erasmus was said to have "laid the egg that Luther hatched."

CHAPTER 3 •

MARTIN LUTHER

In 1513 Niccolò Machiavelli prophetically wrote, "and certainly, if the Christian religion had from the beginning been maintained according to the principles of the founder, the Christian states and republics would have been much more united and happy than what they are. Nor can there be a greater proof of its decadence than to witness the fact that the nearer people are to the Church of Rome, which is the head of our religion, the less religious they are. And whoever examines the principles upon which that religion is founded, and sees how widely different from those principles its present practice and application are, will judge that her ruin or chastisement is near at hand." [1] Four years later, Europeans were made aware that the agent of that chastisement was the Augustinian monk of Wittenberg named Martin Luther.

EARLY YEARS AND ENTRY INTO THE MONASTERY

Martin Luther was born on Nov. 10, 1483, in the town of Eisleben, Thuringia, a region in central Germany. His father, of peasant origin, was a miner with high ambitions for his son. Luther's education at home and at schools in Mansfeld, Magdeburg, and Eisenach was in the usual medieval tradition except for his training for one year at Magdeburg, where he was taught by teachers humanistically educated in the schools of the Brethren of the Common Life. In 1501 he entered the renowned University of Erfurt; there he studied the liberal arts and received his bachelor of arts degree late in 1502. His master of arts degree was obtained in February 1505.

In his theological training at Erfurt, Luther was much influenced by the Occamism of his professors, by the emphasis they placed on the Scriptures, and by their attacks on the Aristotelianism of Scholasticism. Luther began the study of law, a parental decision. Then, while returning from a visit to his parents early in July 1505, he was so frightened by a thunderbolt that struck close to him that he called in terror to the patron saint of the miners, "Help, dear Anne, I will become a monk!" Although his friends tried to dissuade him, Luther entered the Black Cloister of the strict Hermits, or Eremites, of St. Augustine at Erfurt on July 17. The entry into the monastery was probably the culmination of an inner struggle he had been experiencing for some time.

In September 1506, Luther professed the irrevocable vows of chastity, obedience, and poverty. He became a priest the next spring and celebrated his first Mass with awe. In the fall of 1508, Luther was transferred to the Augustinian monastery at Wittenberg to teach at the university recently founded there by Frederick the Wise, the elector of Saxony. While there, Luther also continued his theological studies. Recalled to Erfurt late in 1509, his teaching there was interrupted during the winter of 1510−11 by a trip to Rome on business of the order. Later, at Wittenberg, he received his doctorate (1512), the funds being supplied by the elector. He then succeeded John von Staupitz, vicar of the Augustinian order, as lecturer in Biblical theology.

LUTHER'S INNER STRUGGLE

It was during these years of graduate study and teaching that Luther experienced the inner struggle that was profoundly to affect the history of the Christian church. The Occamism of his training had stressed God's absolute will in the acts of salvation or damnation and yet admitted that there was a possibility that man could contribute to his salvation by his own will. The sensitive and devout Luther could never reach confidence in the sufficiency of his own love for God because of his despair at the awful justice (righteousness) of a stern and demanding God. He feared that he fell short of the perfection which God demanded, because his own love of God did not merit God's love for him. He wondered whether he didn't belong to those predestined to damnation. He imposed upon himself the most rigorous discipline. He read widely among the medieval theological writers and noted their divergence from Scripture. He sought aid and comfort from the sympathetic Staupitz, who was not only his superior but also his father confessor. All to no avail; Brother Martin's sense of sin and unworthiness was too strong. His entire religious background had stressed Christ as the Judge, not the Savior, of the world. Much later in life he confessed: "I was often terrified at the name of Jesus. The sight of a crucifix was like lightning to me and when his name was spoken I would rather have heard that of the devil, because I thought I must do good works until Christ because of them became friendly and gracious to me." [2]

LUTHER'S GREAT DISCOVERY

At Wittenberg, instead of resorting to the customary discussions of the traditional commentaries on it, Luther lectured on the various books of the Bible themselves. His own notes, where extant, and those of his students show a new spirit and a growing, bold dependence on the Scriptures alone and an abandonment of the widespread allegorical approach. His fresh approach won him great popularity as a teacher.

Luther's lecture notes reveal the depth of his inner struggle which centered on the problem of justification, or of God's righteousness, or justice. *Justitia* is the Latin term for the justice of God by which He judges men, either in righteous wrath or in saving mercy.

It was probably in 1514 while he was studying the meaning of Rom. 1:17, "For therein [in the Gospel] is the righteousness of God revealed from faith to faith; as it is written, The just shall live by faith," that Luther experienced his historic discovery. He felt as though he "had entered Paradise through widely opened doors" when he suddenly realized that God loves sinners and judges the believer in mercy, acquitting him from his sin and imputing to him by pure

grace the righteousness of Christ. That is, God justifies the
believer for Christ's sake and by faith alone. Man's moral
deeds play no role in it. Faith, that is, trust in God, is the
"receiving hand" which enables man to accept God's mercy;
it is the instrument of his justification. Although unacceptable
in himself, he is now "righteous" in God's sight and saved.
Faith simultaneously leads the Christian to a life of gratitude
for God's unmerited love.

In the light of this discovery, which Luther found in
St. Paul, the entire late medieval concept of God had to be
reexamined and, along with this, all that was called Christianity. The Gospel, which shows God's mercy through
Christ, became the center of Luther's new theology, a theology that was drastically to change so much of the Christian
church of his day. Yet, so far, Luther was unaware that his
new understanding of the Gospel would revolutionize and
split the church.

Many of the staff and students at the university were
won to Luther's new theology, and the Augustinian's reputation went far beyond the little university town of Wittenberg. Luther, firmly convinced of the truth of his views,
also gradually became more critical of his own Scholastic
theological inheritance, many of the traditional Christian practices, and clerical leadership. Already in 1516 he
preached against the abuses in the indulgence traffic which
subordinated repentance in life to penance, or satisfaction,
which, in turn, was taken care of by the purchase of an
indulgence letter. It was his concern for the dangers that
lay in the use of indulgences that thrust Luther into full
visibility in 1517.

THE INDULGENCE CONTROVERSY

In 1513 Prince Albert of Brandenburg, a young man
without theological training, was named archbishop of
Magdeburg and bishop of Halberstadt. Since this involved
pluralism, the illegal holding of more than one position in
the hierarchy, and since Albert was only 23, not yet 30 as
required by canon law, Pope Leo X granted the necessary
dispensations to Albert for a good sum of money. The

ambitious Albert then also obtained from the pope the more important position of archbishop of Mainz, primate of Germany. A large fee of over 23,000 ducats was required by the papal court for this arrangement. Money to pay part of this fee was borrowed by Albert from the Fugger banking house. To help the new archbishop raise the required funds, Leo X proclaimed an indulgence to be offered to those who contributed to the rebuilding of St. Peter's Basilica in Rome. The papal agreement called for Albert to sell the indulgences in his three ecclesiastical territories and in Brandenburg. When expenses had been paid, one half of the proceeds was to go to Albert's debt with the Fuggers and the other half to Leo.

The archbishop carefully instructed his indulgence agents so as to secure the greatest number of sales. Among these agents was an unscrupulous Dominican monk named John Tetzel, a veteran salesman who employed extravagant language in his sales talk. Tetzel, according to contemporary accounts, was well versed in sales psychology and was credited with using the questionable ditty "As soon as the money clinks in the chest, the soul flits [from purgatory] into heavenly rest" to stress the efficacy of his wares.

The elector of Saxony had not permitted the sale of this indulgence in his lands because he was concerned about any competition to his own remunerative, indulgence-granting collection of relics housed in the Castle Church at Wittenberg. But Brandenburg was not far distant from Wittenberg, and some of the citizens secured indulgences from Tetzel. Luther, as father confessor in the town church, soon became aware of and disturbed by the effect Tetzel was having on the penitential practices of his parishioners who in place of repentance substituted the indulgence letter.[3]

THE NINETY-FIVE THESES

In February 1517, Luther preached a sermon against the false security felt by the holders of indulgence letters. He found indulgences opposed to his new theology that grace alone and no satisfaction on man's part can bring salvation. He decided to open the whole matter to an academic

debate. Late in October, "out of love and zeal for the eluci-
dation of the truth," he drew up 95 theses, or propositions,
dealing with penance and indulgences in general, all of
which he was prepared to debate at Wittenberg or through
correspondence. On October 31, Luther nailed his printed
Latin theses to the door of the Castle Church, the bulletin
board of the university. The date was important, for Novem-
ber 1 was All Saints' Day, and on this festival the elector's
large collection of relics was displayed in the church. Visi-
tors who venerated these relics and made the appropriate
prayers received indulgences. Luther even respectfully
sent a copy of his theses to Archbishop Albert.

The theses were not intended as a protest against the
church, and yet with them the Reformation started. The
first two theses set the tone: "When our Lord and Master Jesus Christ said, 'Repent,' he willed the entire life of
believers to be one of repentance. This word cannot be
understood as referring to the sacrament of penance, that
is, confession and satisfaction as administered by the clergy."
The indulgence cannot take the place of the penance, the
repentance required of the sinner. In other theses he questioned the pope's power to remit all penalties and wondered
why the pope did not use his own wealth to build St. Peter's,
instead of the money collected from the poor. If the pope
could "empty purgatory" for money, why did he not do it
out of charity? Luther did not reject papal indulgences at
this time, but rather he warned of the dangerous misunder-
standings and the extravagant claims for papal power current
among the purchasers and preachers of indulgences.

The effect of the theses was astonishing. They were
translated into German and soon circulated everywhere.
The Dominicans lined up with Tetzel against Luther and his
fellow Augustinians. No wonder the unsuspecting Leo X referred to the controversy in Germany as a "monks' squabble."
A pamphlet war began, a medium of controversy that was
to expand immensely. In October 1518, at the Diet of Augsburg, Luther appeared before the Cardinal Cajetan, the
papal legate who had been ordered to declare the monk
a heretic and summon him to Rome. Luther thought that
the cardinal was as fit to deal with the case on theological

grounds "as an ass was to play a harp." Luther refused to recant his views, and an interview brought no reconciliation.

THE LEIPZIG DEBATE

Luther's next public debate took place at Leipzig in July 1519. Johann Eck, professor of theology at Ingolstadt, was his able opponent. The meeting had originally been planned as a debate with Andreas Karlstadt, a colleague of Luther's, although it was obvious to all that Luther was really the opponent. The basic point of contention was Luther's assertion that the papacy was of recent and human origin. Luther studied the medieval papal decretals, or epistles, in preparation for the debate, and this only convinced him that the papacy was the Antichrist, that is, an institution opposed to the true Christian doctrine. Eck cited ancient authorities, now regarded by all as false documents, in support of the divine origin and thus the primacy of the Roman papacy. Luther doubted the validity of these statements, and in this he was far ahead of his time. Luther was more familiar with Scriptures than Eck, but the latter knew the medieval theological traditions better than Luther. Eck very cleverly forced Luther to declare that John Hus, a condemned heretic, had held views that were "plainly Christian and evangelical" and that the general councils of the church, taught to be infallible, had often erred and "contradicted each other." Luther boldly asserted that "A simple layman armed with Scripture is to be believed above a pope or a cardinal without it. . . . For the sake of Scripture we should reject pope and councils." [4]

The Leipzig Debate settled nothing, of course; but Luther had been pushed farther along in his opposition to the Roman Church. In June of 1520 a bull of excommunication against Luther was issued at Rome. It ordered him to recant or appear in Rome within 60 days. On December 10, Luther publicly burned the bull, an act which was a dramatic closing to a year which had seen Luther's maturing views find expression in three famous and revolutionary tracts.

THE TREATISES OF 1520

Luther's *To the Christian Nobility of the German Nation* was a patriot's appeal to the German princes to throw off the bonds that subjected them to Rome.[5] Luther denied that there was any distinction between the laity and the clergy. Every Christian was a member of "the priesthood of all believers" through baptism. All Christians were responsible for the spiritual welfare of their neighbors and should carry out reforms so that the true faith could flourish. Luther also declared that every Christian had the essential right to read and interpret God's Word. In the priesthood of all believers and in the right of interpretation, Luther was not a religious individualist who felt that everyone should preach, give the sacraments, etc., but rather that each Christian had this potential if properly trained and appointed to the office of the ministry. He thus destroyed the unscriptural medieval distinction between the clergy and laity.

In other parts of *To the Christian Nobility,* Luther asserted that Christian laymen and especially the princes should exercise their Christian duty and power by calling a council to reform the church. He also fiercely denounced the worldliness of the clergy, the drain of money from Germany, and the corruption in Rome. He suggested the formation of a German national church and strongly proposed that the clergy should be permitted to marry so as to eliminate the immorality that so often marked clerical celibacy. He further advocated educational, social, and moral reform. He called for the suppression of the mendicant orders and for the elimination of canon law.

Luther replied to the bull of excommunication by issuing a second revolutionary treatise on Oct. 6, 1520, entitled *The Babylonian Captivity of the Church,* written in Latin and intended for theologians. Here Luther attacked the entire sacramental and sacerdotal system of the Roman Church, which he felt had held Christian souls captive for over a thousand years. Only three sacraments — Baptism, the Lord's Supper, and possibly penance — met the requirements of having promises of Christ attached to them and so were the only real sacraments. The other four sacraments of the Roman Church—confirmation, matrimony, the anointing of the sick, and ordination—however worthwhile, were not sacraments conferring salvation and were not from Scripture.

To Luther, Baptism was really a continual process of "the drowning of the old man" and the coming forth of the "new man" in Christ throughout life. It was an agreement by which God promises forgiveness of sins to the penitent Christian all life long. This lifelong effect and significance of baptism had been forgotten in late medieval Christendom. Luther, unlike some of his more radical contemporaries, upheld the baptism of infants.

In the Lord's Supper, Luther rejected the late medieval doctrine of transubstantiation whereby the substance of the bread and wine were taught to be transformed into the body and blood of Christ. He did, however, take the words of institution literally, asserting that Christ was received by the communicant in the physical elements of this sacrament which, like Baptism, was a covenant (promise, or testament) of God. He denounced the late medieval practice of withholding the cup from the laity and, most importantly, he denied that the Mass (Eucharist) was a meritorious action, a sacrifice or offering of Christ by the officiating priest. Christ's death on the cross was the one sufficient sacrifice for the sins of all ages. Man can do nothing and needs to do nothing to "merit" God's grace and favor. Throughout this manifesto, which raised cries of horror from his opponents, Luther emphasized the role of faith in salvation and the priesthood of all believers.

As for the sacrament of penance, Luther felt that "strictly speaking" this was not really a sacrament, because it lacked an essential visible symbol. The rite had been much abused, for current practice had removed from it the most important elements of repentance and the unconditional nature of God's forgiveness, or absolution, and had stressed instead the church-imposed satisfaction, in which no faith was required.

Late in 1520 Luther wrote a conciliatory letter to Leo X and accompanied it with a calm and edifying pamphlet entitled *The Freedom of a Christian* (see Appendix, No. 3).

The Reformer considered this work a summary of Christian life. He began with a paradox: The Christian man is through faith a free lord and subject to no one; the Christian is the most dutiful servant of all and subject to everyone. That is, the Christian is freed by God's grace from guilt and the need for perfect fulfillment of God's law. However, the believing, regenerate Christian wants to and is obliged to do good works which aid his neighbor. He has no vested interest in doing them, as he isn't earning his way to heaven by them. He cannot *help* but love his fellowman; "Good works do not make a good man, but a good man does good works; evil works do not make a wicked man, but a wicked man does evil works. . . . as Christ also says: 'A good tree cannot bear evil fruit, nor can a bad tree bear good fruit.'" A Christian, loving God and his fellowman, will strive for social improvement by participating actively in community life.

THE DIET OF WORMS

The new Holy Roman emperor, Charles V, summoned his first diet to meet at Worms early in 1521. Yielding to the demands of electors and the people, he granted Luther a letter of safe-conduct for a hearing before the diet, something the Reformer had long requested. The trip from Wittenberg to the city on the upper Rhine River was a triumphal march, and sympathetic crowds came to see and hear the defiant monk. On April 17, Luther appeared before the assembled nobles, clergy, and representatives of the free cities. When asked to identify certain books as his and to recant the heresies in them, he acknowledged his authorship of the books but asked for time to consider the second demand. When the allotted 24-hour delay was over, Luther again appeared before the diet. When asked to recant, Luther pointed out that no simple answer was possible, as he had written on a variety of things, some of which were truly Christian and in defense of the Word of God. He asked to be corrected on the basis of Scriptures. Then, after being asked for a clear and simple answer, Luther made his historic response: "Unless I am convinced of error by the testimony of Scripture or by clear reason. . . . I cannot and will not recant anything, for it is neither safe nor honest to act against one's conscience. God help me. Amen." Still defiant and uncompromising, Luther left Worms on April 26. In the Thuringian forest, by previous arrangement, men of Frederick the Wise spirited the soon-to-be-outlawed monk away to the seclusion and safety of the Wartburg Castle near Eisenach.

THE EDICT OF WORMS

When the emperor had gained from the diet a promise of aid against his enemy Francis I of France and after many representatives of the states had left, Charles submitted and secured the passage of the Edict of Worms, which falsely charged that Luther had written books in which "he destroys, overturns and abuses the number, arrangement and use of the seven sacraments . . . and in astonishing ways shamefully pollutes the indissoluble bonds of holy matrimony . . . . He desires also to adapt our customs and practice in the administration of the most holy sacrament of the holy Eucharist to the habit and custom of the condemned Bohemians. . . . He not only holds the priestly office and order in contempt, but also urges secular and lay persons to bathe their hands in the blood of priests; and he uses scurrilous and shameful words against the chief priest of our Christian faith, the successor of St. Peter and true vicar of Christ on earth. . . . Indeed, he writes nothing which does not arouse and promote sedition, discord, war, murder, robbery and arson, and tend toward the complete downfall of the Christian faith." Since Luther was accused of all these and many other things, the emperor declared that Luther should hereafter "be held and esteemed by each and all of us as a limb cut off from the Church of God, an obstinate schismatic and manifest heretic." Everyone was to refuse Luther "hospitality, lodging, food, or drink." Luther was to be placed in custody and held for punishment.[6] The break with the past was definitive.

AT THE WARTBURG
AND THE RETURN TO WITTENBERG

Luther relieved the boredom of his seclusion at the Wartburg by study and voluminous writing. He wrote a series of sermons so as to give some direction and unity to the preaching of the "new theology" being done under the name of "Lutheranism." Late in 1521 he submitted for publication a Latin work *On Monastic Vows,* in which he attacked the monastic system and the vows taken by the regular clergy. He left it up to the individual whether to leave the monastery or not. He felt that monastic vows were unscriptural and that they rested on the false assumption that there was a special religious vocation, or calling, for certain Christians. Rather, Luther extended the concept of a divine calling to *all* worthwhile occupations. Even the common laborer could exemplify the Gospel in his work.

Luther's greatest literary contribution to the Reformation during his stay at the Wartburg was the translation of the entire New Testament from the Greek to German. His translation, accomplished in only three months, demonstrated his gift for languages and showed that he fully understood the message and the spirit of Scriptures. Its great genius was that it made the New Testament speak in the plain and natural language of the people. It did not read like a translation. There had been numerous German translations before Luther's, but these had not been from the Greek and tended to be wooden and stilted. The book appeared in September 1522 and was immediately a bestseller and an effective medium for the spread of a more Biblical piety among its thousands of readers.

Luther's stay at the Wartburg was disturbed by news from Wittenberg, where his zealous and overenthusiastic associates were pushing the Reformation toward impulsive radicalism. As the violence increased and the spirit of reform took forms alien to Luther's thinking, he left the security of the Wartburg and returned to Wittenberg. On March 9, 1522, he began a series of eight sermons in the town church in which he preached moderation and restraint and the abandonment of reform through force. The preaching of God's Word would achieve the reform; "I will preach it, teach it, write it, but I will constrain no man by force, for faith must come freely without compulsion."[7] Luther always stressed that matters of the spirit can never be forced on anyone. He pointed out that besides the fundamentals of religion, there were many marginal things concerning which man could make a choice. Images, ceremonies, symbols, vestments, festivals, fasts, and other outward customs could be useful in devotion, provided they were not worshiped or regarded as binding the conscience. The Christian was free with regard to them and only had to avoid offending his "weaker brother." There was no iconoclasm in the Lutheran Reformation, and conservatism of this kind was to mark Luther's views for the rest of his life.

BAPTISM AND CONFIRMATION

While changes came gradually, simplified rites and ceremonies were developed in the Lutheran Church. In 1523 Luther retained but translated the traditional order of Baptism. At this time he abbreviated the exorcism and placed the Creed in a later position in the ceremony. He retained the exsufflation (blowing), the sign of the cross, the salt, the spittle on the finger in touching the ears and nose, the prayers before the church building, the holy oil, and the lighted candle. In 1526, however, Luther responded to some efforts at revision by others and to his own evangelical spirit, now more developed, and issued the German *Order of Baptism Newly Revised.*[8] This was a major revision, not only in form but also in spirit. The rite of baptism, administered in the vernacular, was thoroughly abbreviated; all the complicated ceremonial items were deleted and some of the prayers changed. In this service the sponsors renounced the devil and professed the articles of faith on behalf of the infant. Baptism was by triple immersion, a practice which Luther strongly favored. However, pouring water over the head of the child was also practiced in the early Lutheran Church. Luther also retained the use of the white christening robe, which was placed over the naked infant immediately after it had been baptized by immersion. Like Roman Catholicism, the Lutheran Church permitted lay baptism as valid in emergencies. Indeed, the right of baptism was especially given to midwives.

Since confirmation was considered a sacrament supplementing Baptism by the Roman Catholic Church, Luther at first was strongly opposed to such a rite and did not draw up a formula for confirmation. Children were admitted to Communion without it. However, by the time of his death, there were many theologians who advocated the use of an evangelical version of the ceremony. Many Lutheran districts practiced a private confirmation in which the young catechumen was brought by his sponsors to the pastor for examination. If the youth showed sufficient knowledge of Christian doctrine, he was admitted to Communion. Gradually, public confirmation became the general practice, but the actual rite was left up to the individual minister.

COMMUNION

Despite the pressures for radical changes in the Mass and the Communion service, Luther's conservative nature is very evident when he wrote in 1523 his Latin *Formula of Mass and Communion for the Church at Wittenberg*.[9] In it he explained that he had not proposed great changes as he was always hesitant and fearful because of the weak in faith, from whom the old and accustomed order of worship is not to be taken away suddenly. While he retained much of the old form, preserving the old unity and harmony of the service, it became a vital expression of the evangelical faith. Because of the all-sufficient and unique sacrifice on Calvary, Luther deleted the sacrificial elements of the old mass. His whole emphasis was on establishing a simple personal ministration by the sympathetic pastor and a ceremony based on the Gospel, instead of the elaborate rite which purposed to gain God's forgiveness through what was done. Luther felt strongly the reality of God's grace in the historic Christian church and so aimed to discard only the abuses and corruption of the medieval centuries.

As far as the actual rites and ceremonies were concerned, Luther recognized the right of individual choice.

In the matter of consecrating and receiving the bread and wine, the one indispensable thing was that the words of institution be clearly audible, central, and uncorrupted. Private masses, when no congregation was present, were to be discontinued; these were as absurd as preaching God's Word to an empty church. However, announcement of intention to commune was required so that the minister had an opportunity occasionally to examine the communicant as to his understanding of the sacrament and his fitness to partake of it. The use of private confession and fasting was left to the individual. The bread and wine were to be elevated and the bell struck at the consecration, but the people were to be instructed through vernacular sermons that this was not so much for adoration but to remind them of Christ's words of institution. Both the bread and wine were to be distributed to the communicants who gathered as a group before the altar at the beginning of the Communion liturgy. In this *Formula* there was no pressure to use the vernacular, and much of the service remained for the time in Latin, although vernacular hymns were included. The use of the customary and often elaborate vestments was left free; Luther himself at first continued to use the historic attire, but later he varied. After he discarded the monk's garb, he liked to use his academic gown.

In the early Lutheran Church the Lord's Supper was celebrated every Sunday, and the highly liturgical *Formula,* soon paraphrased into German, greatly influenced the Communion service throughout Lutheranism. However, even more popular than the *Formula* was the simpler *German Mass and Order of Service* issued by Luther in 1526.[10] Here the service is in the form of a vernacular paraphrase of the liturgy, and the congregation is made a constantly active participant. Luther did not intend that all Lutheran congregations in Germany adopt this new service; it had originally been intended for use in the homes of the people. He stressed that the German service was pedagogical in nature and was for the "uneducated" laity. In order to have a "chaste and orderly approach," the Reformer thought it best that the communicants come to the altar and kneel, "not men and women with each other but the women after the men, wherefore they should also stand separately at allotted places."

MARRIAGE

Luther rediscovered for the church the high dignity of marriage, which had become obscured by the stress on the celibacy of monks and clergy. Luther's rite for the marriage ceremony was quite similar to that of the medieval Christian church, but he regarded marriage and the married estate as "worldly business," subject to civil and not ecclesiastical jurisdiction. He was quite willing to "permit every city and land to continue its own use and custom." Even though he did not consider the rite a sacrament, he did suggest that the traditional banns be read from the pulpit prior to the wedding and that prayers be said for the betrothed couple. His proposed evangelical ritual (1529) retained the actual marriage in front of the church building. There the vows and the rings were exchanged and the wedding ceremony took place. Then, before the altar inside the church, prayers were said by the minister and the newly married couple were exhorted with Scripture and then blessed.[11]

HYMNS

The spirit of the new theology was perhaps best expressed in the new hymnology that Lutheranism produced. The Lutheran Church became the "singing church," and Luther contributed materially as a hymn-writer to this development. In the desire to enhance the evangelical service, Luther himself composed a large number of vernacular spiritual hymns for congregational singing. Twenty-four of his hymns appeared in 1524 in the first Lutheran hymnal. In the preface to this booklet, Luther wrote of the singing of spiritual hymns as "a goodly thing and pleasing to God." The Reformer desired that the children should be taught these hymns first; then they could lead the congregational singing and assist the adults.

These early hymns were arranged in four parts, Luther tells us, because he desired "the youth, who certainly should and must be trained in music and other proper and useful arts, to have something whereby they may be weaned away and freed from the love ballads and worldly songs, and instead of these learn something wholesome and beneficial, and take up good things with enthusiasm, as is proper for the youth. Furthermore I am not of the opinion that all arts are to be cast down and destroyed on account of the Gospel, as some fanatics protest; on the contrary I would gladly see all arts, especially music, in the service of Him who has given and created them." Many of the hymns that came to be sung by Lutheran congregations retained the fine musical heritage of the medieval church with the texts translated, purged, or expanded, as Luther explained in 1542, to set forth "the living, holy Word of God, to sing, to praise, to glorify with the same, so that this beautiful ornament, music, may in proper use serve her dear Creator and His Christians so that He be praised and honored thereby, but we, through the Holy Word united with sweet song, may be incited and confirmed and strengthened in faith."[12]

CONCLUSION

Although much work was still to be done in rebuilding the structure of a reformed Christian church, the firm doctrinal and liturgical foundation had already been laid by Luther. He had begun his attack on abuses as a loyal son of the church with no intention of creating separate institutional forms. Yet the Reformation of Luther was not a reform of externals, and so it struck at the very heart of medieval doctrine, practices, and institutions. For, when seen in the light of his new Gospel-based theology, much of the vast superstructure that the medieval church had erected on the foundations of early Christianity had to be cleared away. Luther thus rejected the traditions of purgatory, the cult of saints and relics, Mariolatry, the meritoriousness of pilgrimages and fasts, the primacy of the pope, the Mass as a sacrifice, a majority of the seven sacraments, monasticism, celibacy of the clergy, the distinction of the clergy as a separate "spiritual estate," and many other practices and beliefs that in his view had no basis in Scripture and hindered and obscured the true message of the Gospel. And that message centered on salvation as effected by Jesus Christ alone. In his search for the basic doctrines of the pristine church of the early Christian centuries, Luther reaffirmed Paul's teaching of justification by faith alone, instead of by faith *and* good works. By placing the Bible in the vernacular in the hands of all, he emphasized the Biblical basis of Christianity and suggested that all tradition must be in harmony with Scripture. In his revision of the service, he properly stressed the glad tidings of God's love, the heart of his theology. Since the hierarchy of his day was not ready for such radical changes, Luther had to be expelled from the Roman Church, and thus an independent evangelical church had to come into being.

Notes and References

1. *Discourses* I. xii.
2. Roland H. Bainton, *The Age of the Reformation*, Anvil Book 13 (New York: D. Van Nostrand Co., 1956), p. 94.
3. The letter is translated in Henry C. Vedder, *The Reformation in Germany* (New York: Macmillan Co., 1914), p. 44, n. 2.
4. As translated in Roland H. Bainton, *Here I Stand: A Life of Martin Luther* (New York, Nashville: Abingdon-Cokesbury Press, 1950), p. 117.
5. Translated by Charles M. Jacobs in *The Christian in Society I*, ed. James Atkinson, *Luther's Works*, American Edition, 44 (Philadelphia: Fortress Press, 1966), 115–217; see also B. J. Kidd, *Documents Illustrative of the Continental Reformation* (Oxford: Clarendon Press, 1911), pp. 63–65; and E. G. Schwiebert, *Luther and His Times: The Reformation from a New Perspective* (St. Louis: Concordia Publishing House, 1950), pp. 466–73.
6. Translations of the edict can be found in Hans J. Hillerbrand, *The Reformation: A Narrative History Related by Contemporary Observers and Participants* (New York and Evanston: Harper & Row, 1964), pp. 95, 98–100; and in Vedder, pp. 418–27.
7. *Sermons I*, ed. and trans. John W. Doberstein, *Luther's Works*, American Edition, 51 (Philadelphia: Muhlenberg [Fortress] Press, 1959), 77.
8. The orders of 1523 and 1526 are translated in *Works of Martin Luther*, VI (Philadelphia: A. J. Holman Co., 1932), 193–209; and in *Liturgy and Hymns*, ed. Ulrich S. Leupold, *Luther's Works*, American Edition, 53 (Philadelphia: Fortress Press, 1965), 95–103, 106–109.
9. *Works*, VI, 65–117; *Luther's Works*, 53, 15–40.
10. *Works*, VI, 151–89; *Luther's Works*, 53, 51–90.
11. *Works*, VI, 217–30; *Luther's Works*, 53, 110–15.
12. *Works*, VI, 284, 290; cf. *Luther's Works*, 53, 316, 328.

CHAPTER 4 •

LUTHERANISM

Although the Diet of Worms had placed Luther under the imperial ban and in danger of execution, neither the pope nor the emperor were in any position to proceed against Luther and enforce the edict. Popular unrest had been increased by the action at Worms, and many German nationalists felt that Luther must be protected. Many, like Frederick the Wise, wanted a fair treatment for the professor of Wittenberg even though they may not have accepted his new theology. Also, despite the ferment within his empire, Charles V had begun in 1521 the first of his four wars with France. He was too deeply involved with political matters to execute the Edict of Worms and destroy the widening number of Luther's followers.

POLEMICAL LITERATURE

The Edict of Worms did not prevent the energetic Luther from advancing the cause of his evangelical reform whenever and wherever he could. He and his supporters engaged in a pamphlet war with those who were attacking him with violent and abusive language—and often with little understanding of his theological views. Polemical literature was exchanged with many, and all these numerous works, often written in the vernacular, helped spread the new theology to an eager and ever wider audience. Indeed, it is difficult to exaggerate the importance of printing for the spread of the Reformation.

INSTRUCTIONAL LITERATURE

More constructive for the cause of the Reformation was the instructional literature which flowed from the pen of

the busy Luther. There was a desperate need to give some
theological unity to the reform movement by such writings
and to instruct the numerous preachers, often self-called
and unlearned, who were arising in response to their interpretation of the "priesthood of all believers." Luther himself
published a number of sermonets, but most important for
the emerging Lutheran Church was the publication of the
entire Scriptures in Luther's German translation and of the
two catechisms of 1529. The Reformer had completed the
translation of the New Testament while at the Wartburg,
and this was published in September 1522. It is estimated
that 200,000 copies were sold in the first 12 years. Work
was then begun on the more difficult and longer Old Testament, the German translation of which began to appear
serially from 1523 on. The complete German Bible, including
the Apocrypha, appeared in 1534 with 124 woodcut illustrations. This great prose work had a tremendous effect on the
later development of the German language. It made readily
available the all-sufficient source of the faith of the evangelical
movement.

Another instructional work resulted from an official
church inspection, a so-called visitation, of the churches
in Saxony in 1528. Luther saw such "deplorable destitution"
and ignorance that he was constrained to prepare a simple
catechism as an aid to the pastors and heads of families
for the Christian instruction of their congregations or
households. He found that the common people, especially
in the villages, knew nothing at all of Christian doctrines
and that many pastors were quite unfit and incompetent
to teach. Yet all were called Christians, had been baptized,
and enjoyed the use of the sacraments, although they knew
neither the Lord's Prayer, the Creed, nor the Ten Commandments. Using questions and answers, Luther presented
the fundamentals of Christianity in the Small Catechism
in a simple and easily understandable way. It was intended
that after preliminary instruction in the contents of the
Small Catechism the pastors would impart to their congregations a "richer and fuller knowledge" by using the Large
Catechism he also prepared. The value of the German

Bible and the two catechisms in spreading the Gospel, the good news of God's unmerited love, which was the heart of the new theology, is immeasurable.

SEPARATION FROM THE KNIGHTS AND HUMANISTS

After the Diet of Worms, it became necessary for the Reformation to assume its own character and to separate itself from those discontented elements who had different goals and did not really belong in the movement, although they had their usefulness as temporary allies. The earliest separation was from the German knights. This decadent class of feudal society was feeling acutely their loss of prestige as military men, of income in the face of rising prices and an urban economy, and of political power to rising absolutism. During the early years of the Reformation, the knights, strongly nationalistic, hailed Luther as a German patriot who, like themselves, was fighting for liberty from a restrictive and unreasonable foreign (Roman) authority. But the first attempt to use the Reformation in support of social and political reorganization ended in complete failure as the princes everywhere in the German states strengthened their position over the knights.

Another and more serious separation that occurred soon after Worms was from the humanists. Long before the rise of Luther to prominence, northern humanists had appealed for a religious reformation. Although strongly anticlerical, they had hoped for reform from within the constituted lines of ecclesiastical authority. Luther felt a great debt to these humanists who had prepared the way for the Reformation and, by their philological studies and their emphasis on going back to the "sources" of Christianity, had opened up the literature of the early Christian church. As long as Luther attacked the abuses in the externals of religion, such as the indulgence traffic, the humanists supported his bold stand. After the Diet of Worms, however, and with the further development of the new theology to a definite break with Roman Catholicism, many of the humanists deserted Luther. They were reformers but not revolutionaries. Moreover, the humanism that stressed the dignity and essential goodness of man could not really fit into a Christianity that emphasized the total depravity of man and his absolute dependence on God's grace.

The separation of humanism from the Reformation is best seen in the case of Erasmus, who was at first sympathetic to Luther's desire for reform. However, the violence of the attacks on medieval dogma and on the hierarchy by the fiery and energetic monk of Wittenberg was against his gentle nature, and he disapproved of the schism within Christianity that he saw would result. At last, yielding to pressure from both sides, he abandoned his neutral position and wrote his *Discourse on Free Will* against Luther's theological position. In this work Erasmus, averse to dogma, approached the problem of man's ability to act on his own as a humanist. Although he did not completely understand Luther's theological distinctions regarding the subject, he concluded that the denial of the existence of free will on man's part was a dangerous doctrine and incompatible with reason. "I prefer," he wrote, "the opinion of those who attribute something to free will, but a great deal to grace." Without the free will to choose the good, he felt man would be relieved of all moral responsibility.

In reply to the moderate discussion of the problem by Erasmus, Luther published his *Bondage of the Will* in 1525. Here he condemned Erasmus for his rationalist scepticism, vacillation, and inconsistencies. He presented his views again that "the will, having lost its freedom [with original sin], is compulsively bound to the service of sin, and cannot will anything good." Man is either driven by Satan or led by the Spirit of God, and he is saved solely by grace, through faith. Christian doctrine is not based on rational deduction, but on God's revelation in Scripture. By 1525 the separation was complete.

PHILIPP MELANCHTHON

While many of the humanists found it more congenial to their spirit to remain in communion with Rome, a number assisted in the development of Lutheranism. The most significant contribution by a humanist was made by Philipp

Melanchthon (1497–1560). This brilliant young classical scholar came to Wittenberg in 1518 to teach Greek at the university. He entered into a warm and lasting association with Luther, to whom he was deeply devoted. He assisted the Reformer in many ways, including the translation of the Bible into German. In 1521 he published the first edition of his *Loci communes,* or "Common (Scriptural) Passages"; a German translation and revisions appeared later. This apt and systematic formulation of evangelical beliefs based on the chief passages of Scripture was to become basic to the Lutheran movement. Luther, the stormy petrel, and Melanchthon, the quiet scholar, worked well together, although the humanistic scholar often tended to compromise with opposing camps. When Luther died in 1546, Melanchthon acquired the role of leadership in Lutheranism, a task for which he was not fully suited.

PEASANTS' REVOLT

Within a few years after Worms, Luther was forced to show that his reform was religious in nature and that it was not to be identified with the schemes of social revolutionaries. The complaints of the peasants—new oppressive taxes, the introduction of Roman law in the place of the customary feudal law, unjustifiable payments and services to the feudal lords, rising prices, economic monopolies, inferior political and social status, etc.—were of long standing, and the peasants had revolted before. However, the general tensions and ferment in Germany, the new evangelism with its misinterpreted "liberty" of the Christian man, and the obstinacy of the powerful princes, who refused to give any concessions to the peasants, created a situation that erupted in violence. Luther, quite naturally, was hailed as a fighter for freedom, and the peasants erroneously identified his cause with political, economic, and social change. Although some groups espoused the more moderate *Twelve Articles* drawn up as a program at Memmingen early in 1525, in general the revolt was a leaderless and programless uprising. It grew more violent as time went on and the demands of the peasants

were not met. The destruction of monasteries and castles
was great, but eventually the princes, with the aid of German
troops released by the emperor's victory at Pavia in February,
suppressed the revolt, generally with great cruelty. The position of the peasant was debased and that of the princes
enhanced.

Luther, of peasant stock himself, sympathized with the
lot of the peasants and criticized the lords for their oppres-
sion. Yet he feared anarchy and was basically a conservative.
When the *Twelve Articles* were sent to Luther and others for
arbitration, Luther wrote an *Admonition to Peace in Response
to the Twelve Articles.* He felt that the social and spiritual
realms were entirely separate; they were "two kingdoms."
A Christian prince or any duly appointed magistrate should
govern with justice, but Christian subjects should rather
suffer injustice than take justice in their hands. The powers
that be have their authority from God. When the revolt
increased in violence, Luther wrote an inordinately out-
spoken and virulent pamphlet, *Against the Thievish, Murderous
Hordes of Peasants* (May 1525), in which he called upon the
princes to use their God-given authority and put down the
anarchistic rebels with all the cruelty necessary.[1] Later he
wrote several more tracts explaining his views on rebellion
and condemning those who continued to repress the peasants.

The Peasants' Revolt and its cruel suppression had
heavy consequences for the Reformation, for the disheart-
ened peasantry turned from Lutheranism to the more radical
sects. Lutheranism ceased to be a popular movement. Many
princes were likewise estranged from it or hardened against
it because the revolt seemed to confirm their fears that a
change in religion could only result in unrest, anarchy,
and chaos. Lutheranism and rebellion seemed synonymous
to them. Luther's own prestige as a leader of the people
suffered, for his attitude alienated the lower classes. Luther
himself, equally conservative in nonreligious as well as
religious matters, distrusted the peasants thereafter and
relied more and more on the authorities for support and
leadership in the Reformation churches. The Lutheran
churches became "territorial," i.e., governed by the authorities

of the different territories and cities. The people and the local congregation ceased to have anything to say in church government.

LUTHER MARRIES

It was also in 1525, on June 13, that Luther, then 41, married Katharina von Bora, 26, an escaped nun. The decision to follow his own advice that clergy should marry was unexpected even by himself. It caused consternation among his friends, including Melanchthon, and scandalized his enemies. The motives which led Luther into marriage are not well documented. He probably felt that his anticelibacy writings would gain force only if he himself followed his conclusion. He certainly needed a helpmate to take care of the needs of his busy life and to maintain a well-ordered homelife. Undoubtedly he also was sorry for "Kathie," who had deserted the cloister in response to his condemnation of the monastic vow of celibacy and who had previously expressed her willingness to marry him. The union was a happy one and produced six children, two of whom died young. Luther's marriage decisively settled the question about marriage of the evangelical clergy, and the Protestant parsonage was to become a great influence in the Protestant churches and cultures.

THE DIETS AT SPEYER AND "PROTESTANTS"

While Lutheranism spread and grew strong, the political authorities in Germany did little, and Charles was much too busy waging war against France to visit his empire. In the diets held at Nürnberg in the period 1522−24, the princes showed their fear of a popular revolt if they attempted to enforce the Edict of Worms which had banned Luther and his supporters. Instead they called for a general church council and for reform of the Roman Catholic hierarchy. At the Diet of Speyer in 1526, with the emperor still absent, the strength of the Lutheran princes present resulted in a call for a national church council to be held in Germany. It was also decided by a recess, or concluding act, that as far as the enforcement of the Edict of Worms was concerned, each German ruler should so "live, govern and carry himself as he hopes and trusts to answer to God and his imperial majesty." This compromise meant mutual toleration and territorial control of religion. But three years later, when the diet again assembled at Speyer, the Roman Catholics held a firm majority over the disorganized Lutheran princes. Following the demands of the still absent emperor, the estates acquiesced to his illegal abolition of the recess of 1526.

Meanwhile, when the aims of the emperor were becoming all too clear, the elector of Saxony, the margrave of Brandenburg, the duke of Lüneberg, the landgrave of Hesse, and the prince of Anhalt, along with the representatives of 14 free cities, some of them Zwinglian, presented a strong written protest.[2] In this document the signers protested that what had been unanimously agreed upon at the Diet of Speyer in 1526 could not legally be rescinded even by majority vote. While pledging political obedience to the emperor, they asserted that in those matters which "concern the glory of God and the welfare and salvation of souls" they were pledged in baptism to hold God's Word above temporal authorities. They also felt that they must state their grievances and "protest [witness] and testify openly before God" and all men that if these grievances were not accepted by the emperor, they would all "consider null and void the entire transaction and the intended decree" as being "against God, his holy Word, all our soul's salvation and good conscience," as well as the recess of Speyer. By this brave and religiously oriented pledge, the "protesting" estates unwittingly bequeathed the name Protestant to all who left the Roman Catholic Church.

THE AUGSBURG CONFESSION

The emperor ignored the "protest" and called for a diet to meet at Augsburg in 1530. The Protestant princes now feared suppression by force and sought to unite in a political and military union, but the theological differences between them could not be overcome. It was in these troubled times, some suppose, that Luther wrote his great hymn "A Mighty Fortress Is Our God." Charles arrived at Augsburg—his first visit to Germany since 1521—and the atmosphere was decidedly unfavorable for Protestantism. On June 25 the Lutherans read to the diet a confession prepared by Melanchthon which presented the basis of their faith and their views on such controversial practices as clerical celibacy, monastic vows, and the giving of the cup to the laity. The Lutherans tried to show in this document that they were not innovators, but faithful to the ancient faith of the whole church. An attempt by Melanchthon to win over the traditionalists was very evident in this Augsburg Confession and in the discussions that followed. Despite the conciliatory tone of the confession, the "Catholics," which term was now becoming the exclusive name for the papal adherents, contemptuously rejected the Lutheran confession as well as the more radical confessions prepared by four South German cities. However, the Lutherans did not swerve from their confession, and the Augsburg Confession became the standard of Lutheran doctrine everywhere.

It was soon evident that the religious issue was to be determined by the use of force, and the Lutherans and other Protestants united in the League of Schmalkalden. Confronted by a stronger opposition than before, the emperor and the Catholic princes could do nothing to coerce the Protestants. In 1532 the Peace of Nürnberg was negotiated as a truce until a general council would be held. Charles V was busy with his wars and negotiations, and religious colloquies between the Catholics and the Protestants accomplished nothing except to give the latter more time to expand.

LUTHER'S DEATH

Luther died on Feb. 18, 1546, at the age of 63. This great man of God had in his lifetime wrought a tremendous change in the Christian church through his courage, his creative mind, his preaching and writing ability, his own deep faith, and his personality. Despite frequent illness and great demands and pressures, Luther had restored the

Gospel to the hands and hearts of the people, had over-
thrown doctrines and practices which were contrary to
Scripture, and` had restored the Pauline teaching of justifi-
cation by faith alone. It was his tragic role at this juncture
of history to destroy the unity of the medieval church, a role
which was largely forced on him by the opposition rather
than chosen. Rome had not yet awakened to the need for
a genuine reform of Christendom, and when the awakening
came, the lines of division had already become hardened.

WAR AND PEACE

By 1546 Charles was at peace with France, and within
a few months of Luther's death he began a war against the
Schmalkaldic League. Although the Protestants had superior
forces, they lacked leadership and unity. Wittenberg fell
on May 19, 1547, and the league soon collapsed. The vic-
torious Charles did not demand, however, that the conquered
Protestants return to Roman Catholicism; he still hoped to
secure religious unity through negotiation and a truce.

The final formulation of a religious settlement was
made at the Diet of Augsburg in 1555. The Religious Peace
of Augsburg concerned only the Catholics and the followers
of the Augsburg Confession, the Lutherans. Its provisions
excluded the Calvinists, the Zwinglians, and the Anabaptists.
These confessions were barred and were to remain illegal
in the empire until 1648. The peace officially recognized
the principle that religious unity within the political community was necessary for its solidarity; the princes and the
free cities had to choose between Roman Catholicism and
Lutheranism. All subjects within a principality were required
to conform to the official religion or emigrate. Religious
minorities in the free cities were to be tolerated, though
not receiving official status. Thus the religion of the government determined the religion of the subject—*cuius regio,
eius religio* ("whose region, his religion"). The religious peace
also provided for an "ecclesiastical reservation": if a Catholic
spiritual ruler of an ecclesiastical territory, like a diocese,
should become a Lutheran, he was to be deposed and his
territory would remain Catholic under his successor. Thus

no new ecclesiastical lands were to become Protestant, but all such church estates confiscated by the Protestants before 1552 were to remain in the hands of the new owners. Despite the limitations and the later violations of these provisions, peace was maintained on this basis for more than half a century.

TERRITORIAL CONFESSIONS

The Peace of Augsburg meant that the Lutheran princes assumed episcopal (bishoplike) authority over their territories and administered church affairs through consistories, or tribunals, made up of both clergy and laymen of high status. Instead of the church being supreme over the state as was so often the case in medieval Christendom, the Lutheran churches were now organized under state superintendents, officials of the government. Separate territorial confessions resulted. With the strong guidance of Luther gone, the Lutheran theologians in Germany became partisans of different factions. This tore German Lutheranism apart. Conflicts within Lutheranism and conflicts between Lutheranism and the growing Calvinism greatly weakened the position of Protestantism before the forces of the Counter Reformation. An end to the bitter theological bickering was finally achieved with the Formula of Concord in 1580, which laid the basis for unity of doctrine in the Lutheran Church in Germany and clearly differentiated the Lutherans from the Calvinists.

LUTHERANISM OUTSIDE THE EMPIRE

The Lutheranism that spread in the German states after 1521 soon took root in other countries. Luther's works were read widely throughout Europe, and the students who flocked to the University of Wittenberg from many non-German lands brought Luther's theological views back with them to their homeland.

The Scandinavian countries to the north were among the earliest to accept the Reformation. In Denmark, Biblical humanism had prepared the way for the evangelical movement that developed. King Frederick I (1523–33) separated the Danish church from Rome and with the aid of Hans Tausen, his chaplain, carried out other reforms. When Christian III (1536–59) came to the throne, the Reformation was accelerated, although often for political reasons. In 1536 a national assembly introduced Lutheranism as the state church with the king as the supreme head. The crown seized what ecclesiastical property had not already been appropriated by the nobles. Luther approved the new church ordinance that was introduced in 1539 as the basic law of the Danish state church, and later the Augsburg Confession was adopted. Danish translations of the New Testament appeared in 1524 and 1529, the latter the work of Christian Pedersen. The first complete Danish Bible was published in 1550.

Norway, which was under Danish rule, followed the example of Denmark, although the Reformation there was not a popular movement. Only slowly was Lutheranism accepted, for the Bible and other religious literature were available only in Danish. A Norwegian church ordinance was not proclaimed until 1670. Christian III also attempted to introduce the Danish ecclesiastical system into Iceland, but progress was slow.

Sweden revolted against the rule of Denmark in 1521, and the national hero Gustavus Vasa was elected king of an independent Sweden in 1523. The ties that bound the Swedish church with Rome were soon cut, and reforms along Lutheran lines were introduced. Sweden's greatest reformer was Olavus Petri. He had studied at the University of Wittenberg during the years when Luther was experiencing his own theological development. Petri became a preacher of Lutheranism in Stockholm. He also married. The Swedish translation of the New Testament which was published in 1526 was largely his work. Like Luther's German translation, this and later vernacular versions of the Bible were of great importance in developing a national language and a Bible-based religion. In 1527 the Diet of Västerås destroyed the privileged position of the Roman church and legalized the preaching of the Reformation. The king proceeded to confiscate the wealth of the church, and in 1536 the Swedish church officially became evangelical (Lutheran) and a national church. Sweden's reformation was most conservative. It kept the office of the bishop and developed a rather rich liturgical life. In 1541 appeared the first Swedish translation of the entire Bible, the work of a commission which included Olavus Petri and his brother Laurentius. The latter had also studied at Wittenberg and was archbishop of Sweden. Comprehensive church ordinances were published in 1571. Finland, under Swedish rule, followed the example of Sweden in its reformation and acceptance of Lutheranism.

In the Baltic states the Reformation rapidly gained ground after 1520 among the German population in such cities as Riga, Reval (Tallin), and Dorpat (Tartu). The Order of the Teutonic Knights, ruler of most of the region, also joined in the reform movement. Evangelical preachers spread Luther's views everywhere, and church ordinances soon were introduced. Andreas Knöpken was the leader of the evangelical movement in Riga. In 1554 the Diet of Wolmar officially declared for the Reformation, but political dissolution came soon after the middle of the century when the scattered areas were absorbed by the neighboring states. However, Lutheranism continued to flourish.

The Reformation also had notable success in Eastern Central Europe, although the pattern of development was different in these regions where there were no strong monarchs, where the noble landlords dominated the feudal populace, and where cities and towns were few and of little importance. The anti-Roman influence of the Eastern Orthodox Church was also strong in some areas, although this church, spiritually separated from Rome, did not become involved in the Reformation. In the areas of Poland, Bohemia, and Hungary with subject Slovakia, the ground for the Reformation had been prepared by humanism. To a lesser degree, schismatic Hussitism also prepared many to accept the new Protestant ideas being spread by visiting merchants and returning students.

In Poland there existed a definite need for a reformation of the church and the hierarchy. There were the usual complaints about the loss of national wealth to Rome, the greed of the clergy, and the authority of the distant pope. The views of Luther, and later of Calvin, as spread by preachers, found acceptance in the towns and among the lesser nobility, but there was no mass secession from the Roman church. In 1555 the national diet declared religious freedom, but the arrival of the Jesuits in 1564 turned the tide back to Catholicism in Poland. Strong Lutheran, Calvinist, and Unitarian minorities persisted, however, into the 17th century.

In Bohemia, the home of Hus, the Reformation was welcomed first by the German-speaking population, and Luther's many acknowledgments of his debt to Hus also led to friendly relations between the Czech Hussites and the Lutherans. Although the Neo-Utraquists, led by their Lutheran members, and the Bohemian Brethren united in a common confession of faith to present a united front in their struggle for religious liberty, the Hapsburg rulers' counterreformation policies eventually suppressed the Reformation in Bohemia.

Lutheranism also found acceptance among the Germans and Slovaks of Hungary and Transylvania, where considerable religious freedom was possible amid the political confusion that reigned after the disastrous victory of the Turks at Mohács in 1526. An early preacher of Luther's views was Mátyás Dévay, a humanist who had studied at Wittenberg. The New Testament was translated into the Magyar language. After the middle of the century, many of the Hungarian nobles and gentry gradually became more attracted to the non-German, logical, and republican Calvinism with its presbyterian system. They, in turn, superimposed their Calvinism on their subject peasants. In the 17th century the Jesuits were able to regain most of the people of Hungary for Catholicism.

Notes and References

1. An English translation of Luther's tract against the peasants is given in Henry C. Vedder, *The Reformation in Germany* (New York: Macmillan Co., 1914), pp. 427–31.
2. For the protest at Speyer see Vedder, pp. 431–40.

CHAPTER 5

ZWINGLI AND THE
RADICAL REFORMATION

Considering the extent of the desire for reform in the Christian church in the early 16th century, it was to be expected that other leaders besides Luther and new varieties of Protestantism would appear independent of the German reformation emanating from Wittenberg. The second major reform movement was to be the work of a German-Swiss named Zwingli and was to center in Zurich.

ULRICH ZWINGLI

Ulrich Zwingli was born in the Swiss village of Wildhaus on Jan. 1, 1484. He was thus only two months younger than Luther. After receiving a good humanistic education at the universities of Vienna and Basel, he was ordained a priest and took a pastorate at Glarus. During his 10 years at Glarus he continued his humanistic studies, corresponded with his idol Erasmus, and even enjoyed for a time a papal pension as a reward for supporting propapal political activities. Twice he acted as chaplain for Swiss mercenary troops campaigning in Italy. In 1516 he removed to Einsiedeln and, although he had been critical of corruption in the church before, it is here that he began, as a reforming humanist, his attacks on indulgences and other abuses. Then in December 1518 he was called as preacher and pastor to the Great Minster (cathedral) of Zurich, where he took up his new duties on his 35th birthday, Jan. 1, 1519.

It was not long before Zwingli started his reformation in this thriving city, which was also a center of Biblical humanism. He immediately began an ambitious series of vigorous sermons on the books of the New Testament, though with emphasis and interpretation more Erasmian than Pauline. Early in 1519, with the support of his bishop, he secured the recall of an indulgence seller. Later that year, after Zwingli had recovered from the plague, an illness that provoked a great deal of introspection and soul-searching, his reforming activities increased. Taking encouragement from Luther's open demands for reform, Zwingli preached against the Lenten fast, monasticism, purgatory, and sacerdotal celibacy as unscriptural. Then on Jan. 25, 1523, in a public disputation that was to be the first of three, Zwingli defended 67 theses, or propositions, he had drawn up. These, unlike Luther's, covered a wide range of topics. They stressed the importance of the Gospel and the sufficiency of Christ's atonement for salvation, and they attacked celibacy, the Mass as a sacrifice, purgatory, food restrictions, and other externals not sanctioned in the New Testament. Zwingli condemned the Roman Catholic hierarchy for their negligence and warned them of the consequences.

CHANGES AT ZURICH

With the full support of the city council for the innovations, the reformation at Zurich accelerated. The council ordered in June 1524 that "there should be no more playing of organs in the city and in the churches; no ringing for the dead, and for and against the weather; no more blessing of palms, salt, water, and candles; and no more bringing to anyone of the last baptism or extreme unction; but that all such superstitions should cease and be clean put away, inasmuch as they are all at variance with the clear word of God." [1] Images were destroyed by iconoclastic enthusiasts, the monastic houses were dissolved, and priests married. Zwingli himself married Anna Reinhard, his companion of many years.

The last Mass was celebrated in Zurich on Wednesday of Holy Week in 1525, after which the altars and sacristies were stripped. This was not done without the disapproval of some, for "what pleased one man well did not please his neighbour." Zwingli then introduced a new order of service. On Maundy Thursday the young people who desired to partake of the Lord's Supper placed themselves on the "floor of the nave between the choir and the entrance, males to the right and females to the left." Upon completion of the sermon, unleavened bread and wine, in "trenchers and beakers . . . of wood, that no pomp come back," were placed on a table set on the floor of the nave. After the words of institution were recited "openly and intelligibly, in German," the bread was carried on large wooden platters from person to person so that each communicant could "break off a bit or a mouthful with his hand and eat it." In the same way the wine was distributed; "and no one shall move from his place." The custom of going up to the altar to commune was thus discontinued, and sitting at Communion received an indirect start. After "open and clear" words of praise and thanksgiving, the congregation responded with an "Amen." On Good Friday the middle-aged worshipers communed in a similar manner, "men and women apart." On Easter Sunday the old folks partook of the Lord's Supper. This order of the Communion service was to be followed at Easter, Pentecost, autumn, and Christmas.[2] On ordinary Sundays a preaching service, without liturgy or singing, was held.

Later, when it was observed that the people were not attending services but wandering "hither and thither during sermon-time, on the bridges, down the alleys, by the gates and alongside the moats," the city council ordered in the summer of 1531 that "every man shall strictly observe the mandate to go to Church on Sundays and Holy-days." To obtain better supervision, it was also ordained that "the preachers in all the three churches shall begin to preach at one and the same time, convenient to all." They also decreed that "the morning sermon shall take place every day, as hitherto, and that at 8 a. m. for half-an-hour there shall be a discourse and prayer."[3]

ZWINGLI COMPARED WITH LUTHER

Many of Zwingli's doctrines and practices were similar to those of Luther; yet there were also marked differences. The Zurich reformer accepted the basic creeds of Christianity, and with Luther he emphasized the unique and all-sufficient role of Christ's atoning death and of faith for salvation. Like the reformer of Wittenberg, Zwingli relied solely on Scripture and rejected papal and conciliar authority, sacerdotal celibacy, purgatory, the possibility of human merit before God, the veneration of images and saints, and monasticism. In Zurich too, the need was felt for a Bible in the language of the people, and Leo Jud translated the Scriptures into the Swiss-German dialect (1534). Unlike the Lutheran Reformation, however, the movement at Zurich was strongly legalistic and iconoclastic. The Bible was the unique source not only of doctrine but also of all church practice there. The externals of the religious life were not left free but had to be prescribed in the New Testament or done away with. With the great emphasis on the intellectual exposition of the Word through instruction and the sermon and because of the lack of available hymns in the vernacular, music in worship was at an end. The service on an ordinary Sunday was not based on the Mass, and the people played no active part in it.

Zwingli had no feeling for the sacraments as the means of grace. The Spirit did not use physical means in Zwingli's understanding, so heavily influenced by his humanistic-philosophical training; "We must distinguish between the bread which is received by the mouth and Christ who is received by faith." [4] The sacraments, separated from faith, are simply signs of spiritual realities existing independently from them. So the bread and wine of the Eucharist were not the body and blood of Christ, but only symbols commemo- rating Christ's passion. They expressed the fellowship of Christians and indicated that the recipient was a member of a Christian society. To Zwingli, Baptism meant little more than initiation of the Christian into membership in a reli- gious society. Because of this, he was quite willing to have infants baptized. The divergence from Luther's sacramental theology prevented the two reformers from reaching an accord when they met at the Marburg Colloquy in 1529.

ZWINGLI'S DEATH

From Zurich, a town now virtually a theocracy because of the close association of church and state, the Zwinglian reformation spread to Bern, Basel, and other Swiss cantons. Opposing them were the Catholic cantons which resisted the spread of the new doctrines and Zwingli's attempts at political leadership in the Swiss confederation. In 1529, on the burning of a missionary from Zurich in the Catholic canton of Schwyz, Zurich and her allies declared war. No battle occurred, however, and the First Peace of Kappel was negotiated between the opponents. It was decreed that since "no man ought to be forced in matter of faith . . . neither side shall make war upon nor chastise the other for its faith." The districts that had abolished the Mass and done away with images were not to be punished, and where the Mass and other ceremonies were retained the people were not to "be subjected to force, nor shall any preachers be sent, appointed, or assigned to them, so long as the majority objects."[5] This statement constitutes the first gleam of tolerance in the darkness of traditional religious intolerance.

The peace was only a truce, for in 1531 the Protestant allies sought to compel the Catholic cantons to permit the preaching of reformed doctrines in their territories. When this was refused, an economic blockade was instituted by the Protestant league, an act which led to war. The Catholic army of 8,000 men met the Protestant army of only 1,500 at Kappel on Oct. 11, 1531. Zwingli accompanied his forces as chaplain, and he was among the 500 Zurichers killed in the defeat. Luther considered Zwingli's death an example of God's rightful judgment of those who take the sword to defend the Gospel.

In the Second Peace of Kappel, the Swiss cantons were divided along religious lines. Zurich and her allies, in return for freedom to practice their form of worship, agreed to allow the Catholic cantons, seven in number, to "abide without any contradiction or dispute, in their true undoubted Christian faith, now and hereafter, throughout their cities, lands, territories, and lordships, all evil devices, evasions, deceit, and fraud being dismissed and put away."[6] Heinrich

Bullinger succeeded Zwingli, and in 1536 he and others drew up the First Helvetic (Swiss) Confession. In 1566 the Zwinglians united with the Calvinists on the basis of one confession, the Second (revised) Helvetic Confession, in the Reformed Church.

THE RADICAL REFORMATION

The Marburg Colloquy of Luther and Zwingli was not the only demonstration that the Reformation was not to be a homogeneous movement. Despite their initial approval of Luther, many others besides Zwingli soon found that for various reasons they must desert the Wittenberg reformer. In their unbounded enthusiasm for the new evangelical movement, they envisioned more radical changes than the conservative Luther allowed and thus were disappointed in the Lutheran reformation and even with the more radical happenings at Zurich. Despite a multiplicity of views as to how to restore a true and pure Christianity, all the radicals opposed the close association of church and state that was identifiable in the major churches of their day. Usually these dissidents wanted to free the Christian church of the medieval accretion of ecclesiastical traditions and magisterial (civil) power and to restore, resurrect, or re-create the kind of church that had existed in primitive Christianity. Just how this was to be done was widely debated, but often the scheme included community ownership of property. Because these heterogeneous groups held views of the church that were more radical than those of Luther and the other major reformers, they have been labeled "the left wing of the Reformation."

ANABAPTISM

The word *Anabaptism* comes from Greek and means "to baptize again." As a general term, it was applied to all those who did not accept infant baptism as Scriptural and thus rebaptized adults. Baptism to them, as to Zwingli, was not a means of grace. In their view, baptism was a sign of faith and repentance and only an adult was capable of believing and of feeling need for the newness of life. Although there were great variances among them, the Anabaptists were Zwinglian in their interpretation of the Lord's Supper. Whereas the other reformers saw themselves standing within the ongoing lifestream of historic Christianity, the Anabaptists felt they were starting all over again. The medieval church to them had lost all continuity with the apostolic life and spirit.

Most of the Anabaptists were extremely literal in their interpretation of the Bible, and there was also a tendency among them to stress the words of the Book of Revelation, which they felt especially applied to their times, the end-time of the world. Strongly moral and ethical, they lived exemplary lives marked by simplicity, sobriety, and humility. Most of them repudiated oaths, war, capital punishment, and the union of church and state as found in the political world about them. It was primarily because of their views on these political issues and because of their appeal to the oppressed classes of society that they were persecuted as radical revolutionaries. The cruel punishments visited upon them by Lutheran, Zwinglian, Calvinist, and Catholic public authorities alike only convinced the Anabaptists of the validity of their tenets, for to them the mark of the true Christian church was suffering and persecution. Strongly apocalyptic, they suffered and awaited the coming of Christ. (See Appendix, No. 4)

PERSECUTION

The Anabaptists first arose in Zwingli's own circle of disciples when a group of like-minded humanists and clerics banded together to press for the establishment of a truly apostolic church. Two of the early leaders were Conrad Grebel and Felix Manz of Zurich. Both were to be martyred. Naturally, their rejection of infant baptism and especially their disassociation from the secular and worldly state and society soon clashed with the opinion of Zwingli, who saw a very close association between the state and the church and who thought in terms of a Christian commonwealth, a Christian society. Early in 1525 the Zurich Council decreed that "all those therefore who hitherto allowed their children to remain unbaptized, must have them baptized within the next week; and whosoever will not do this, must with wife and child, goods and chattels, leave our city, jurisdiction, and dominions, or await what will be done with him."[7] Those deported spread their faith wherever they went, for all Anabaptists were zealous in their missionary activities. Sterner action was soon necessary, and in March 1526 the Zurich Council forbade adult rebaptism among the Anabaptists and ordered that "if any one hereafter shall [re]baptize another, he shall be seized by our Lords and, according to the decree now set forth, will be drowned without mercy."[8]

By the time of Zwingli's death, the number of Anabaptists in Switzerland was negligible. But the movement had spread throughout the German states, to the horror of the Lutherans and Catholics. In 1528, Emperor Charles V made rebaptism punishable by death, and the next year the Diet of Speyer decreed that all unrepentant "Anabaptists and rebaptized persons, male or female, of mature age, shall be judged and brought from natural life to death, by fire or sword or otherwise, as may befit the persons, without preceding trial by spiritual judges."[9] Although Luther himself was opposed to compulsion in matters of faith, Catholic and Lutheran magistrates united in carrying out this mandate, and many Anabaptists were cruelly executed.

THE MÜNSTER EPISODE

The Anabaptists were quietists for the most part, but in 1534 some radical Anabaptists succeeded in taking over the city of Münster in Westphalia when John of Leiden and John Matthys, two Anabaptist leaders, came from the Lowlands to aid the discontented elements in the city and to lead the citizens to a victory over the forces of the bishop to whom the city was subject. Once in control of the city council, the Anabaptists drove out all who refused rebaptism. They then sought to establish a communistic New Jerusalem of truly baptized believers with the young John of Leiden ruling as "King of Zion" over the elect. Besieged, the city was put on a war economy while the confiscated wealth and luxuries were distributed to all. Because of the numerical superiority of women, polygamy was introduced. The "king" took several wives. Many Anabaptists throughout Europe prayed for the success of the Münster experiment, and some sought unsuccessfully to bring relief to the besieged city. As the danger of revolt in other areas increased, authorities in the empire aided the besieging forces. The starving defenders could not hold out much longer, and the city was taken through treachery. Most of the male defenders were slaughtered with the severity considered necessary to wipe out such a threat to the established social order. John of Leiden was cruelly tortured before being killed.

The Münster episode, besides giving Anabaptism an offensive name and intensifying persecution, led the scattered and despised remnants to renounce all forms of violence and extremism and to live quiet, simple, and inoffensive lives. They became uncompromising pacifists. Menno Simons patiently organized his followers in the Lowlands and North Germany into groups later known as Mennonites; Jacob Hutter in Moravia similarly organized the Hutterite communities. Their descendants still maintain disciplined, austere, and pious pacifist communities in America and elsewhere.

Although not as prominent in theology, organization, and number as the other Christian churches of that day, the groups within the Radical Reformation movement did contribute much to the sharpening of theological studies and argumentation in the Reformation period. By breaking with the commonly held view of the *corpus Christianum* or the unity between the church and society, they influenced Western institutions and life.

Notes and References

1. B. J. Kidd, *Documents Illustrative of the Continental Reformation* (Oxford: Clarendon Press, 1911), p. 443. See also Charles Garside Jr., *Zwingli and the Arts*, Yale Historical Publications, Miscellany 82 (New Haven: Yale University Press, 1966).
2. Kidd, pp. 443–44.
3. Kidd, p. 450.
4. Hans J. Hillerbrand, *The Reformation: A Narrative History Related by*

Contemporary Observers and Participants (New York and Evanston: Harper & Row, 1964), p. 150.

5. Kidd, p. 470.
6. Kidd, pp. 475 – 76.
7. Kidd, p. 453.
8. Kidd, p. 455.
9. Henry C. Vedder, *The Reformation in Germany* (New York: Macmillan Co., 1914), p. 439.

CHAPTER **6** •

JOHN CALVIN

EARLY YEARS AND EDUCATION

Although his name was to be associated most closely with a Swiss city, John Calvin was born on July 10, 1509, at Noyon in northern France. His father, Gérard, was a notary and served as secretary to the local bishop. At the age of 14 the young John, already religiously inclined, entered the ancient and famous University of Paris. Calvin soon showed himself an eager, serious, and able student of theology. In 1528 he received his master of arts degree and on the command of his father turned to the study of law. He also undertook the study of Greek and was strongly influenced by humanism. In 1532 he published, at his own expense, a humanistic and learned commentary on Seneca's book *On Clemency,* a work on political ethics. In it he gave evidence of the humanistic and analytical methods of examination and explanation that he was to follow successfully in his later exposition of Scripture.

THE INSTITUTES OF CHRISTIAN RELIGION

Meanwhile Calvin had been influenced by Reformation thought, although the date of his "sudden conversion" is not known. Then in 1533 Calvin's name was associated with Nicholas Cop, the rector of the University of Paris, who was charged with heresy. Calvin fled first to Noyon, later to Saintonge, and in 1534 he visited the aged humanist Jacques Lefèvre d'Étaples at Nérac. Emboldened by his contact with this courageous reformer, Calvin decided not to accept Roman ordination but to dedicate himself to the task of reform. He became convinced that there could be no genuine reform within the institutional church as it then existed. In 1534 he experienced two brief periods of imprisonment; the persecution of Protestants in France was taking a more serious turn. The next year Calvin appeared in the Protestant Swiss town of Basel. Here, in March 1536, he published his very influential book, the *Institutes of the Christian Religion* (see Appendix, No. 5). It was intended as an expanded catechism. This Latin edition of 1536, consisting of only six chapters and explaining the Decalog, the Apostles' Creed, the Lord's Prayer, the sacraments, and church government, was to be greatly enlarged in the second edition (Strasbourg, 1539) and then translated by Calvin into dignified French (Geneva, 1541).

Rightly considered as a "classical statement of Protestant theology," this work of Calvin is very comprehensive and systematic in its treatment of the whole range of Christian theology. The work shows Calvin's legal training as well as his deep piety. Theologically, the *Institutes* is filled with an awed awareness of the majesty and sovereign power of the almighty God. The Scripture contained for him the all-sufficient, authoritative truth upon which the church rests, as well as the entire pattern of its life.

CALVIN COMPARED WITH LUTHER

Calvin was deeply influenced by Luther, and there were many similarities between the Wittenberg reformer's fully developed theology and that of Calvin. Both were much indebted to St. Augustine in their assertions that man is morally helpless and entirely dependent on God's grace for salvation. Both accepted Scripture as the sole source of Christian doctrine, and both discarded as unscriptural purgatory, the papacy, Mariolatry, the cult of the saints and of relics, the Mass as a sacrifice, monasticism, the celibacy of clergy, and many other medieval developments. Both stressed that any useful secular work is a "calling" from God. Both accepted as true sacraments only those sacred actions that had an explicit "promise of Christ" attached to them:

Baptism and the Lord's Supper. Man was saved only by God's grace through faith; good works were ineffective for salvation.

Despite these similarities, there were also fundamental differences in the theology and practice of the two reformers. Calvin's theology was much more legalistic than Luther's. The latter stressed the God of love as portrayed in the New Testament, a God who so loved the world that He sent His only-begotten Son to redeem mankind. Calvin was more influenced by the Old Testament in his vision of God as the Lawgiver who demanded obedience to His divine precepts. Luther was quite conservative in retaining such customary things as candles, ceremonials, images, altars, vestments, instrumental music, and chanting as aids in creating an atmosphere conducive to the worship of God; Calvin severely rejected everything that did not have express New Testament sanction. It has been said—somewhat unjustly, for Calvin himself desired a rich Communion liturgy—that a Calvinist church consisted of "four bare walls and a sermon." In his effort to explain the Lord's Supper, Calvin, like Luther, believed there is a real partaking of Christ's body and blood in its celebration; unlike Luther, he did not regard them as present in the bread and wine, nor did he accept the ubiquity of Christ's glorified body. To Calvin, Christ's body is in heaven and only the devout communicant spiritually partakes of it through the work of the Holy Spirit. This mystery is such that it is to be experienced rather than explained.

As far as the relation between church and state was concerned, both Luther and Calvin held that the pure doctrine of Scripture must be maintained by public authority. Both reformers felt that God had instituted the temporal power of the state and that resistance to rulers was morally wrong. To Luther, however, the state was strictly a worldly power that could in no way coerce the conscience or soul of a subject. Calvin was opposed to the principle of a union of church and state because he felt that the church authorities should set the standards of orthodoxy and discipline for enforcement by the secular powers. This led to the theocracy at Geneva. As Calvin put it: "Yet civil government has as its appointed end, so long as we live among men, to cherish and protect the outward worship of God, to defend sound doctrine of piety and the position of the church, to adjust our life to the society of men, to form our social behavior to civil righteousness, to reconcile us with one another, and to promote general peace and tranquillity."[1] Luther felt strongly that secular authority was God-given and God-ordained, but he showed no preference for any particular form of government. Since the secular authorities were a "divine order," all men must obey the rules. Calvin, too, considered the office of the magistrate one of the most honored of vocations. He condemned the cruel and impious rulers of all times and warned of the Lord's vengeance upon them. Since private individuals could only suffer and obey such rulers, he urged action by a constituted magistracy "to restrain the willfulness of kings" who "violently fall upon and assault the lowly common folk." He felt that an aristocracy (rule of the best), "or a system compounded of aristocracy and democracy, far excels all others." Men's faults and failings make "it to be safer and more bearable for a number to exercise government, so that they may help one another, teach and admonish one another; and, if one asserts himself unfairly, there may be a number of censors and masters to restrain his willfulness."[2]

PREDESTINATION EMPHASIZED

Much more than Luther, Calvin placed special importance on the traditionally orthodox belief in predestination. Calvin went beyond the view of St. Augustine in asserting a double predestination in which God had not only selected some for eternal life but had also damned all the rest to everlasting damnation. God had from all eternity *willed* the salvation of some and the damnation of others irrespective of merit; He had not used just His foreknowledge of a man's faith or goodness in making these elections, because God's knowledge is not a passive knowing but coincides with His will. Calvin himself called the damnation of some by God's decree "dreadful" but certain, unchangeable, and not to be questioned by puny mortals. Many readers of Calvin's works were repelled by this concept of predestination, for it seemed to make God the author of sin, but to Calvin this example of God's judgments and undeserved mercy was an appalling mystery beyond man's limited understanding.

Since every Christian wanted to know if he was one of those elected to salvation, there developed in Calvinism a tendency to look for possible signs of such selection. Calvin felt that those who publicly professed their faith, partook of the sacraments, and lived a godly life met the test. However, no one could judge the election status of others, he taught. It was also generally felt that the elect would have within themselves not only the inner "witness of the Spirit" and a strong desire to do good, but also an urge to reform the wicked and remove any opportunity for sinning. Calvinism was therefore to be marked by a degree of zealousness and reforming activity, much of it preventive, unknown to other Protestant groups.

CALVIN COMES TO GENEVA

In 1536 Calvin went to Ferrara, Italy, for a brief time and then returned to France during a period of amnesty. Intending to go to Strasbourg, Calvin was detoured by war to Geneva, a Swiss commercial city of about 12,000 inhabitants. A few years before Calvin's arrival, Geneva had turned to Protestantism through the preaching and activities of Guillaume Farel, a provocative, red-bearded, and venturesome evangelist. Although Calvin intended to stay only overnight in Geneva, Farel heard of his arrival and persuaded the author of the *Institutes* to stay by calling upon God to condemn Calvin if he did not devote himself to the work of reform in Geneva. Calvin accepted that as a divine call and, except for a short interlude at Strasbourg, remained in Geneva until his death in 1564.

THE STRASBOURG INTERLUDE

Calvin and Farel set up a system of instruction and pressed for a close relation between citizenship and church membership, the latter based on a creedal test. All citizens were to be subject to a strict religious-moral discipline, delineated by the clergy. In a showdown between the ministers' demands and the city council's support of the more lenient discipline of the nearby city of Bern, Calvin and his associates were forced by the city's General Council to leave Geneva in April 1538. The reformer accepted the call of the Protestant leaders of Strasbourg to come to their city and take charge of the congregation of French refugees there.

This free city on the Rhine had been influenced very early by the writings of Luther and had soon become an important center of reforming activity and a refuge for religious exiles of all kinds. Most influential among the Strasbourg reformers was Martin Bucer (1491 – 1551), who preached and wrote there from 1523 to 1549. This indefatigable humanist worked hard to harmonize the theological differences between Luther and Zwingli at Marburg and on later occasions. Bucer firmly believed that the magistrates should promote reform and supervise the church so as to achieve a moral community. He had very definite ideas about liturgical reform, church discipline, predestination, and education. Since Calvin was a close friend of Bucer and was closely associated with him during a highly formative period of his life, the influence of the Strasbourg reformer on the later theology and ecclesiastical polity of Calvin was great.

For three busy and fruitful years Calvin resided in Strasbourg. Under Bucer's influence he compiled a book of French psalm paraphrases set to music for singing in the services. He also introduced a disciplinary system and a new order of service in his parish. He published his *Commentary on Romans* and a revised edition of his *Institutes*. In August 1540 he married one of his parishioners, but his family life was not as significant and comforting for him as for Luther and Bucer. His wife was sickly and died quite early.

THE ECCLESIASTICAL ORDINANCES

Late in 1540 Calvin was recalled by Geneva, and in September of the following year he reentered that city. He immediately set about drafting a new ecclesiastical polity, the famous *Ecclesiastical Ordinances of the Church of Geneva.*[3] The civil government approved a modified version which did not grant all that Calvin requested but which did place the administration of church discipline in the hands of church officials supported by the state, instead of in the hands of the city council. The document, basic to all later Calvinistic organization, names four divinely sanctioned ministries "instituted by our Lord for the government of his Church." These were pastors, teachers, elders, and deacons.

The pastors, selected on the basis of a test and with the approval of the city government, were to "proclaim the Word of God, to instruct, admonish, exhort and censure, both in public and private, to administer the sacraments and to enjoin brotherly corrections along with the elders and colleagues." The ministers of Geneva and the nearby villages held weekly discussions. In each of the three parish churches there were three services on Sunday and a preaching service on Monday, Wednesday, and Friday mornings. The weekday services were later held daily. Catechism classes for youth were held at noon on Sunday in every parish, and at 16 the young people, baptized in infancy, made their own profession of faith. Communion was celebrated in all three parish churches four times a year, on Christmas, Easter, Pentecost, and the first Sunday in September.

The teachers, or "doctors," were to instruct "the faithful in true doctrine, in order that the purity of the Gospel be not corrupted either by ignorance or by evil opinions." Since instruction in theology was profitable only if the languages and humanities were studied first, "a college should be instituted for instructing children to prepare them for the ministry as well as for civil government." A school for boys was to be set up, but the girls were to have "their school apart, as has hitherto been the case." This stress on education became normative for all Calvinism.

The twelve elders, "men of good and honest life, without reproach and beyond suspicion, and above all fearing God and possessing spiritual prudence," were chosen from and by the city officials. The elders were to exercise "oversight of the life of everyone, to admonish amicably those whom they see to be erring or to be living a disordered life, and,

where it is required, to enjoin fraternal corrections themselves and along with others." If necessary, offenders were
turned over to the city magistrates for punishment.

The deacons, divided into procurators and hospitalers,
were to "receive, dispense and hold goods for the poor, not
only daily alms, but also possessions, rents and pensions,"
and to "tend and care for the sick and administer allowances
to the poor."

NEW ORDER OF SERVICE

In 1542 Geneva adopted with slight modification the
new order of service which Calvin had introduced in the
French parish at Strasbourg.[4] Its Communion part, contrary
to Calvin's wishes, was not to be celebrated every Sunday
but only four times a year. Unlike Luther, who basically
retained most of the old Mass and cut out only its objectionable parts, Calvin wrote a new liturgy, retaining only some
of the structure and elements of the traditional Mass. In his
service he attempted to restore the worship as he felt it had
been in the ancient Christian church. The focal point of
the service was the preaching of the Word. On the Sundays
when Communion was to be celebrated, the intercessory
prayer with a lengthy paraphrase of the Lord's Prayer led
to the Communion rite. A consecration prayer, mostly of
Calvin's own composition, was followed by the words of
institution. In the accompanying exhortation the minister
restricted the Communion to the faithful, a feature that
later came to be known as "the fencing of the tables."

In the exhortation Calvin's theological view of the Lord's
Supper is given in that Christ wishes "to make us partakers
of his own body and blood, in order that we may possess
him entirely in such a manner that he may live in us, and
we in him. And although we see only bread and wine, yet
let us not doubt that he accomplishes spiritually in our souls
all that he shows us externally by these visible signs; in other
words, that he is heavenly bread, to feed us and nourish
us into life eternal." Christ is not in "these earthly and
corruptible elements which we see with the eye, and touch
with the hand," but our souls must be "raised above all

terrestrial objects, and carried as high as heaven, to enter the kingdom of God where he dwells." The people were to regard the bread and wine as "signs and evidence, spiritually seeking the reality where the Word of God promises that we shall find it."

RITES AND CEREMONIES

The rite of Baptism as inaugurated by Calvin differed from that of the Lutheran Church. Since Calvin held that "assurance of salvation does not depend upon participation in the sacraments, as if justification consisted in it," Baptism became in the Calvinistic, or Reformed, church only "a token of our union with Christ." All the "alien hodgepodge" and "theatrical pomp" were discarded. It was of no importance to Calvin "whether the person being baptized should be wholly immersed, and whether thrice or once, whether he should only be sprinkled with poured water." He left that up to the practice of the locality, but he did point out that "the rite of immersion was observed in the ancient church." Baptism of the children of believers, as heirs of God's covenant with the fathers, was retained. It was to be administered only by the clergy, and since it was not necessary for the salvation of a person whose eternal fate had been determined by God, emergency baptism at the home of the infant was not permitted. Under no circumstances should a woman ever administer the rite. The ceremony was confined to the church, before the assembly of believers, to stress the child's membership in the covenant people. No sponsors were required, and no profession of faith was made for the infant.[5]

Confirmation, according to Calvin, should really be a "catechizing, in which children or those near adolescence would give an account of their faith before the church." By studying a manual like Calvin's *Catechism*, a "child of ten would present himself to the church to declare his confession of faith, would be examined in each article, and answer to each . . . while the church looks on as a witness."[6] This procedure became the general practice in the Reformed Church.

The rite of Communion as adopted by the Reformed

Church followed the pattern established by Calvin. The communicants were to announce their intention to commune a week before the celebration so that no unconfirmed child, uninstructed stranger, or newcomer would approach the table "to his own condemnation." The Communion tables were placed beside the pulpit, and there was to be no "large number of vessels." Only a minister or a deacon could give the chalice, and the minister himself received the bread and wine first. Then, "in becoming order the believers should partake of the most holy banquet, the ministers breaking the bread and giving the cup." Calvin left to the local church's discretion "whether or not the believers take it [the bread] in their hands, or divide it among themselves, or severally eat what was given to each; whether they hand the cup back to the deacon or give it to the next person; whether the bread is leavened or unleavened; the wine red or white—it makes no difference."[7] Since Calvin, like Luther, had a deep feeling of the fellowship of Christians in the Lord's Supper, private masses with no congregation present were repudiated.

As for marriage, Calvin felt that the banns should be published in the church for three Sundays prior to the wedding. Marriages could be performed on any day except a Communion Sunday. In the actual ceremony, the couple to be married came forward to the Holy Table at the commencement of the sermon. Before the assembled congregation, after exhortation from Scripture, the bridegroom and bride were married by separately expressing their intention of accepting each other according to God's Word in holy matrimony. The ceremony was concluded with prayer.

THE CONSISTORY

The Genevan Consistory, composed of six pastors and twelve elders, met every Thursday with one of the four city syndics, or officers of the city government, presiding. Although the elders outnumbered the clergy, Calvin's all-pervasive influence and indomitable will were very evident. These alone enabled the consistory to win out in its constant struggle with the city government over the right of the ecclesiastical establishment to control discipline as well as doctrine. For, although the consistory at first confined its disciplinary activity to matters of public morality, it soon extended its functions and control more widely. All sorts of rules and regulations were instituted to make Geneva a saintly city (see Appendix, No. 6). Church attendance was required of all, and Sunday was decreed a day of worship and strict rest. The keeping of Christmas was forbidden as a pagan and Roman Catholic festival. Attendance at secular theatrical productions was forbidden, as were dancing, playing cards, and the singing of bawdy songs. An attempt to close the taverns failed, but they were carefully regulated. Objectionable names were not to be given at baptism, and thus there developed the Calvinistic practice of using only Biblical names. Types of clothing and luxuries were regulated.

Using methods that reflected the spirit of the medieval inquisition, the vigilant consistory gave its judgments. Capital crimes included blasphemy, heresy, witchcraft, and adultery. All who openly opposed the ecclesiastical system and its police in any way were banished. Between 1542 and 1546, records reveal, 58 were executed and 76 banished from Geneva. To the serious and zealous John Knox, Geneva was "the most perfect school of Christ that ever was on earth since the days of the apostles."

During the last decade of Calvin's life, the consistory and the city magistrates collaborated well. Ecclesiastical discipline was tightened, and the international prestige of the reformer grew immensely. Calvinism itself spread, especially after the establishment in 1559 of the Genevan Academy (the University of Geneva today) and through the training of refugees who later returned to their homelands. Under the able leadership of Theodore Beza, the humanist who was to be Calvin's successor, and staffed with brilliant instructors, many of whom were refugees, the academy made Geneva the intellectual and missionary center for Calvinism. At the time of Calvin's death (1564) there were 1,200 junior students in the school and 300 in the higher levels, all receiving their education free of cost. Many of the advanced students were from foreign countries. These returned to their native lands imbued with Calvinistic theology and spirit.

CALVIN'S CONCEPT OF VOCATION

The activistic, aggressive, and dynamic spirit of Calvinism can be attributed in part to Calvin's views on predestination, but his concept of vocation was also important. To Calvin, every Christian acknowledging the role of God through faith also accepted thereby grave responsibilities. No matter what his duties or tasks, the Christian must have a deep sense of dedicated service to God and to his neighbor, also created in the image of God. A layman's work was really not a secular calling; he was doing God's work and was acting as a steward of God with his earthly possessions. Calvin expressed his concept of vocation with these words: "The Lord bids each one of us in all life's actions to look to his calling. . . . he has appointed duties for every man in his particular way of life. And that no one may thoughtlessly transgress his limits, he has named these various kinds of living 'callings.'" Even the very humble tasks were precious in God's sight, and every vocation was hallowed. No vocation was without its troubles, but "it will be no slight relief from cares, labors, troubles, and other burdens for a man to know that God is his guide in all these things. The magistrate will discharge his functions more willingly; the head of the household will confine himself to his duty; each man will bear and swallow the discomforts, vexations, weariness, and anxieties in his way of life, when he has been persuaded that the burden was laid upon him by God. From this will arise also a singular consolation: that no task will be so sordid and base, provided you obey your calling in it, that it will not shine and be reckoned very precious in God's sight."[8] In his views on vocation, Calvin thus took a position similar to that of Luther.

CALVIN AND CAPITALISM

Calvin's views on the Christian vocation, or "calling," and his permission to demand interest on loans of money, limited by equity and charity, have led to a great deal of discussion and controversy as to the role of Calvin and Calvinism in modern capitalism. Some writers, like the German sociologist Max Weber, have advanced the thesis that the "spirit of capitalism" was a kind of by-product of the Calvinist ethic of work and vocation. Some authors have accepted this view, others have modified the thesis as an oversimplification, and still others have rejected it entirely.

Calvin himself certainly insisted on diligence and frugality and condemned the lazy and wasteful man. Writing on stewardship, he pointed out that all Christians should remember "by whom such reckoning is required." He warned against being overly ambitious: "For no one, impelled by his own rashness, will attempt more than his calling will permit, because he will know that it is not lawful to exceed its bounds. A man of obscure station will lead a private life ungrudgingly so as not to leave the rank in which he has been placed by God." Calvin constantly referred to the more miserable condition of the godly who suffered while the wicked flourished. He rejected economic individualism and advocated altruism; the Scripture warns us "that whatever benefits we obtain from the Lord have been entrusted to us on this condition: that they be applied to the common good of the church. And therefore the lawful use of all benefits consists in a liberal and kindly sharing of them with others." [9] In general, it might be said that there was a greater affinity between Calvinism and business than was the case with Lutheranism. And the cradle of Calvinism was in an urban commercial setting, the city of Geneva. The relationship of Calvinism to modern capitalism should not be overemphasized, however.

SPREAD OF CALVINISM

As Calvin attained an international reputation and as his theological views found wide acceptance, Geneva became the capital of international Protestantism. In the Second Helvetic (Swiss) Confession (1566) the Zwinglians were drawn into a common confession with the Calvinists to form what was later to be called the Reformed Church. This confession, published only two years after Calvin's death, won wide acceptance throughout Europe. In the German territory of the Palatinate, the Lutheran confession was replaced by a modified and milder Calvinism based on the

Heidelberg Catechism (1563). This work, drafted by the Calvinistic professors at the University of Heidelberg, became the doctrinal basis for the Reformed churches in Germany, the Low Countries, and even for the Philippists, Lutheran theologians who followed the views of Philipp Melanchthon. Calvinism also spread to Eastern Europe. Here, however, the short-lived centers of Calvinism in Poland fell before the forces of the Counter Reformation. Those in Hungary survived.

CALVINISM IN FRANCE

Even before the Reformation began in Germany, the French church had cut many of the traditional ties with Rome and had become virtually a national church ruled by the French clergy and their king. Anticlericalism and demands for internal reform were still common, however, and influential clergy and scholarly humanists pressed for a spiritual awakening. When Luther's works appeared, they were widely read and discussed despite condemnation. For political reasons King Francis I (1515—47) himself was at times favorable to the Lutherans, for he thought to use the aid of the German Protestant princes in his wars with Charles V. Most frequently, however, and especially when placards violently attacking the Roman Mass appeared in Paris in October 1534, he persecuted the Protestants in France. He saw in the new sect a danger to his control of the church in his realm and feared that disunity based on religious pluralism could only weaken his authority.

The publication of Calvin's *Institutes* in French in 1541 gave theological unity to the French-speaking Protestants. The many French Protestants who had fled to Germany and later to Geneva continued to maintain contact with those who remained in France during the severe persecutions of Henry II (1547—59). Many of these exiles returned after receiving training at Geneva, and Protestantism in France continued to grow under the guidance and encouragement of Calvin. These persecuted French Protestants came to be called Huguenots, a word traditionally derived from the German word for confederate, *Eidgenosse.*

A number of Huguenot congregations were founded about 1555, often by pastors trained in Geneva. Many nobles and persons of the middle class joined these congregations of converts who numbered about half a million and who assembled in defiance of the government's policy of repression. Confident of their growing strength and in the desire to frame church polity and beliefs, about 50 congregations sent representatives to the first synod of French Protestants meeting in Paris in 1559. The influence of Geneva was evident in the polity adopted, although there were of necessity some variations because of the size of France. An elective and representative structure provided for meetings of the pastors and elders in the local consistory of the congregation, in the colloquy representing a number of congregations, and in the provincial synod. The national synod was to meet once a year. Matters of discipline and authority similar to those of the Genevan *Ordinances* were approved. With the adoption of a common confession of faith and polity by the Huguenots, the division between Roman Catholics and Protestants became clear and consolidated.

THE RELIGIOUS WARS IN FRANCE

The political-military strength of the Huguenots was such as to constitute a threat to the Catholic rulers, and civil war resulted. The war began in 1562 with the massacre at Vassy, where troops of Duke Francis of Guise, a powerful and reactionary Catholic prince, killed more than 60 Huguenots whom they found worshiping there. The ensuing bitter struggle was marked by indecisive victories, by assassinations, and by periods of armed truce and toleration. Both sides called in foreign powers, and the original religious issues became confused with political, dynastic, and nationalistic problems.

ST. BARTHOLOMEW'S DAY MASSACRE

About 1570, during one of the periods of truce, the Huguenot admiral Coligny gained considerable influence at the court of King Charles IX (1560—74). It was agreed that the Huguenot leader, Prince Henry of Navarre, should marry Margaret of Valois, the daughter of the queen mother Catherine de Médicis, and thus bring about a union of the two leading families of royal blood, one Huguenot and the other Roman Catholic. But Catherine became jealous of the influence Coligny had on her son, the king. She turned to the Guises, and together they convinced Charles IX that Coligny and his influence must be eliminated. Assassination was to be the method used. The festivities attending the marriage of Henry and Margaret were at their height when an attempt on Coligny's life was made. The Huguenot leader was only wounded, however, and Catherine and the Guises now decided on a mass killing of all Huguenots who were in Paris for the wedding. On the morning of St. Bartholomew's Day, Aug. 24, 1572, the church bells gave the signal and the massacre began. In Paris alone, 3,000 Huguenots were slaughtered, and another 10,000 lost their lives in areas outside the capital. The life of Henry of Navarre was spared. Although Pope Gregory XIII considered the massacre an occasion for thanksgiving, many throughout Europe were shocked at the brutal act.

THE EDICT OF NANTES

The eighth and final war of religion in France ended with Henry of Navarre the acknowledged heir to the throne (Henry IV, 1589–1610). A state of anarchy existed in France, and in order to facilitate his general acceptance as the king of France and to unite the country once again, Henry abandoned his Huguenot faith and became a Roman Catholic, the religion of the vast majority of the French people. His Protestant faith had never meant much to him; he is credited with saying, "Paris is worth a Mass." Using military action, persuasion, and bribery, he won over his remaining enemies and entered his capital in March 1594.

In 1598 Henry IV protected his former Huguenot coreligionists by issuing the Edict of Nantes. Although the edict made Roman Catholicism the official religion of the state, a large share of religious and legal liberty was granted to the Huguenots, who at this time probably numbered over one million from among the nobility and the middle class. Liberty of conscience was given to all Frenchmen, and freedom of worship was granted to those of "the allegedly reformed religion" in all places where it had been practiced for the previous two years, except for Paris and the immediate vicinity. The Protestants were given the same legal rights as the Roman Catholics and were also declared eligible to hold any public office, to enter the universities, schools, and hospitals, and to hold public assemblies. About 200 fortified places were placed in the hands of the Huguenots for eight years as a guarantee that the provisions of this favorable edict would be enforced. Originally declared to be perpetual and irrevocable, the Edict of Nantes was revoked in 1685 by Louis XIV, and persecutions began once again.

Thus, despite the strength of Calvinism in 16th-century France, that country was to remain Roman Catholic. Protestantism could not overcome the consistent opposition of French monarchs who were relatively satisfied with their control over the national church under the Pragmatic Sanction of Bourges (1438) and the Concordat of Bologna (1516). Protestantism had never gained much support among the French peasantry, the vast majority of the French people. Coming much later than the Lutheran Reformation in Germany, French Calvinism met and failed to overcome the counterreformation movement generated by the Roman Catholic revival that had taken place by then.

CALVINISM IN THE LOW COUNTRIES

While the wars of religion were being waged in France, a religious revolution had started in the Low Countries to the north. The 17 provinces that made up the Low Countries were a part of the Holy Roman Empire under Charles V. Again religious convictions formed only a part of the issues that led to war and to a struggle for independence from Catholic Spain. Even though the Low Countries were an early center of mysticism, the condemnation of Luther's works, and the burning of the first Lutheran martyrs (1523), there Protestantism in its various forms gained a firm hold. Persecutions were intensified by the government, especially against the Anabaptists, despite the general unpopularity of such action.

When Charles V divided his possessions and gave the Low Countries to his Spanish-educated son Philip in 1555 and when Philip became the ruler of Spain the next year, tensions increased rapidly in the Low Countries. Philip II failed to understand the temper of the people and the times and offended Catholics and Protestants alike by his appointment of Spanish officials, his demands for money, and his cruel repression of the Protestants, now strengthened by an influx of aggressive Calvinists. Philip left the Low Countries in 1559, but by that time a clash between Spanish rule and the people was inevitable.

WILLIAM OF ORANGE

William of Orange (1533 – 84), a talented Protestant Dutch prince, organized military opposition in the Low Countries against Philip's religious repression and Spanish encroachment on their ancient liberties. Philip's answer was to send the brutal duke of Alva with veteran troops to the Low Countries. Alva's cruelty and the actions of those who succeeded him in command only strengthened William's cause. A temporary union of all the provinces for the expulsion of the hated Spanish troops was achieved in the Pacification of Ghent (1576).

William still hoped to achieve unity among all the provinces, but the religious differences between a Calvinist north and a Catholic south were too great and a permanent division occurred. The seven northern provinces formed the Protestant Union of Utrecht, the basis of the Dutch Republic, while the southern provinces united in the Catholic Union of Arras and supported Spain. The cause of unity and Calvinism suffered a severe blow when William was assassinated in 1584. The war of the Dutch states against Spain dragged on until the Twelve Years' Truce was made in 1609. When hostilities were renewed during the Thirty Years' War (1618 – 48), the United Provinces of the north had a number of allies, and in the Peace of Westphalia its independence was recognized.

The United Provinces was the last European state to be won by Protestantism. The area became known for its vigorous Calvinism, and it was here that many Puritans from England found refuge.

CALVINISM IN NORTH AMERICA

From Europe, Calvinism came to North America with colonists of that religion settling in the New Netherlands, Massachusetts, South Carolina, Pennsylvania, Canada, and elsewhere. The Calvinists came from England, France, the Low Countries, Scotland, and the German Palatinate to establish their ecclesiastical polity, their churches, and their blue laws limiting various kinds of activity. It must be remembered that Pocahontas was baptized by the Calvinist minister Alexander Whitaker and that the only clergyman who signed our Declaration of Independence was John Witherspoon, a Scottish Presbyterian. Calvinism is the soil from which later developed the Congregationalists and Baptists. All British-rooted Protestantism is in some way related to Calvinism.

Notes and References

1. *Institutes* IV. xx. 2; *Calvin: Institutes of the Christian Religion*, trans. Ford Lewis Battles, ed. John T. McNeill, *The Library of Christian Classics*, XX – XXI (Philadelphia: Westminster Press, 1960).
2. *Institutes* IV. xx. 31, 8.
3. *Calvin: Theological Treatises*, trans. and ed. J. K. S. Reid, *The Library of Christian Classics*, XXII (Philadelphia: Westminster Press, 1954), 58 – 72.
4. "The Manner of Celebrating the Lord's Supper" is given in John Calvin, *Tracts and Treatises on the Doctrine and Worship of the Church*, trans. Henry Beveridge (Grand Rapids, Mich.: Wm. B. Eerdmans Publishing Co., 1958), II, 119 – 22.
5. *Institutes* IV. xiv. 14; xv. 19, 20.
6. *Institutes* IV. xix. 4, 8, 13.
7. *Institutes* IV. xvii. 43.
8. *Institutes* III. x. 6.
9. *Institutes* III. x. 5, 6; vii. 5.

CHAPTER 7

THE ENGLISH AND
SCOTTISH REFORMATIONS

The reformation in England had been long in preparation. In the 14th century, waves of anticlericalism had swept the country, Wycliffe had thundered his warnings against the papacy, and the statutes of Provisors and Praemunire had drastically curtailed papal jurisdiction over England. Papal control over the English church became even weaker when the strong Tudor dynasty came to power in 1485 after the War of the Roses. Nationalism had grown during the Hundred Years' War with France, and such feeling came in conflict with the international sway of the papacy. The people of England readily accepted the English translation of the New Testament by William Tyndale, and Luther's works were widely distributed and debated in England. Yet it is doubtful whether England would have made a complete break with the papacy if Henry VIII had not encountered difficulties in securing an annulment of his marriage to the Spanish royal princess, Catherine of Aragon.

HENRY VIII AND REFORM

Henry, well trained in theology and of unquestioned orthodoxy, was perturbed that his marriage with Catherine had produced no male heirs but only a princess named Mary. Since Catherine had been his brother's widow, their marriage had been possible only by papal dispensation as contrary to canon law and certain portions of Scripture (Lev. 20:21). Henry thought God had evidently not blessed the union. A male heir seemed absolutely necessary to perpetuate the dynasty. In 1527, after 18 years of marriage,

Henry requested an annulment from Pope Clement VII. Because the pope feared reprisals from Catherine's powerful Spanish family, he hesitated. Henry decided to take the matter in his own hands. In 1529 he summoned Parliament, and during the ensuing six years this "Reformation Parliament" carried out his plans to sever the English church from Rome. In 1531 the king secured from the clergy recognition as the "Protector and Supreme Head of the English Church and Clergy . . . as far as the law of Christ allows." Parliament next moved against the payment of annates to the pope and by the Act in Restraint of Appeals removed the pope's spiritual jurisdiction over England. In 1533 Henry secured a dissolution of his marriage to Catherine from Thomas Cranmer, archbishop of Canterbury and primate of the English church. The king then married Anne Boleyn, a union that also failed to produce the desired male heir. Their only child was the princess Elizabeth. When the pope excommunicated Henry and declared the marriage of Henry and Anne invalid, and thus their child illegitimate, papal revenues from England were cut off completely. In the Act of Supremacy (1534), Parliament confirmed the king as "the only supreme head in earth of the Church of England, called *Anglicana Ecclesia.*" The act also declared that he should "have and enjoy, annexed and united to the imperial crown of this realm, as well the title and style thereof, as all honours, dignities, pre-eminences, jurisdictions, privileges, authorities, immunities, profits and commodities to the said dignity of supreme head of the same Church belonging and appertaining."[1] It became treasonable to deny the king this position and title. John Fisher, bishop of Rochester, and Sir Thomas More, the author of the famous *Utopia,* were executed for not accepting the king as head of the church. In general, however, the substitution of the king for the pope created little disturbance.

THE DISSOLUTION OF THE MONASTERIES

The supremacy of the king was first exercised in the dissolution of the monasteries of England on the pretext of corruption. The dissolution, a real break with the ecclesiastical past, provided the crown with considerable much-needed money and at the same time eliminated possible centers of propapal feelings. The dispossession of all the monks and friars was carried out with efficiency and little suffering. In 1536 those houses having an annual income of less than 200 pounds were declared dissolved by Parliament, which resolved "that it is and shall be much more to the pleasure of Almighty God and for the honour of this his realm that the possessions of such spiritual religious houses, now being spent, spoiled and wasted for increase and maintenance of sin, should be used and converted to better uses, and the unthrifty religious persons so spending the same to be compelled to reform their lives."[2] In the following years the larger monasteries shared the same fate. Many of the monastic properties were given away by the king or sold at bargain prices to the local gentry, who thus became strong supporters of the king's antipapal policies.

In all the actions taken by Henry and Parliament, political, economic, and national motives had been uppermost. The king was not anti-Catholic; he still considered himself a good Christian in the Catholic tradition and had not instituted any changes in doctrine or services. Lutheran influence was spreading in England, however, and the appearance in 1535 of the Bible in the translation of Miles Coverdale led to open discussion of the issues. By the king's order, an English Bible was placed in every parish church, available for reading by laymen. But Henry was not attracted to Luther's views. In order to secure unity in religion, Parliament, under Henry's guidance, enacted the Act of Six Articles (1539). This reaffirmed the traditional tenets of transubstantiation, celibacy, private masses, auricular confession, and Communion under one element. Persecution of those suspected of Protestantism followed.

EDWARD VI AND CRANMER

Henry VIII died early in 1547 and was succeeded by the young Edward VI, his son by Jane Seymour, his third wife. The Council of Regency was predominantly Protestant, and Edward was educated by Protestant tutors. Under the regency of the moderate Protestant Edward Seymour, duke of Somerset, England began to move along the road of doctrinal and liturgical change. The Act of Six Articles and the statutes against heresy were repealed. In 1549 an Act of Uniformity required the use of the First Prayer Book in the churches of England. This book, largely the work of Archbishop Thomas Cranmer, provided new services in place of the customary Latin Mass and the monastic "hours." It was written in beautiful English and drew much on these traditional services as purged by the Lutheran Reformers. However, Cranmer, unlike the Lutheran Reformers, did not merely translate and purge the old Latin texts. He was a creative liturgical writer himself. His phrasing allowed for considerable latitude of interpretation. The services centered on the Psalms, Scripture readings, and appointed collects in an attempt to return to the ancient services of the Christian church in a condensed, simplified, and purified form. In the Lord's Supper, both the bread and the wine were given to the communicants: "Graunt us therefore (gracious lorde) so to eate the flesche of thy dere sonne Jesus Christ, and to drynke his bloud in these holy Misteries, that we may continuallye dwell in hym, and he in us, that our synfull bodyes may bee made cleane by his body, and our soules washed through hys most precious bloud."

The English Reformation was deliberately conservative and conciliating so far, but under the growing influence of Bucer and the Swiss, iconoclasm now began in England. Altars and images were removed from the churches. Marriage of the clergy was legalized. When the duke of Northumberland overthrew Somerset in 1549, Protestantism moved more rapidly towards the Reformed types. This was aided by the arrival in England of a number of religious refugees from the continent. The Second Prayer Book of Edward VI, again produced by Cranmer and made compulsory by the Second Act of Uniformity (1552), was more Zwinglian in tone. Vestments were abolished, and the Lord's Supper was to be received primarily "in remembrance." It was stressed that the Mass was not a sacrifice, since Christ by His death on the cross had "made there (by hys one oblacion of hymselfe once offered) a full, perfecte and sufficiente sacrifice, oblacion, and satisfaccion, for the synnes of the whole worlde, and dyd institute, and in hys holye Gospell commaund us to continue, a perpetuall memorye of that his precious death, untyll hys comynge agayne."[4] Congregational participation was limited to the litany; there was no singing of hymns. In the six years of Edward's reign, England moved gently and with no Catholic martyrs from Catholicism to Reformed Protestantism. However, the English Reformation, imposed as it was from above, was suddenly brought to a halt by the death of Edward in July 1553.

MARY TUDOR AND THE CATHOLIC REACTION

By law, Edward's successor was Mary Tudor, the daughter of Henry and Catherine of Aragon. Mary was passionately Roman Catholic, and Parliament acceded to her wishes by repealing almost all of the religious statutes that had been passed since 1529. It would not restore the confiscated church lands, now in the possession of many of its members, or recognize the supremacy of the pope. As her demands increased and when she even married Philip of Spain, the heir to the throne of a country that was fast becoming England's major enemy, Mary's popularity declined rapidly. Persecutions of Protestants began in 1555, after Parliament had revived the heresy laws. The martyrs burned at the stake numbered about 300 and were drawn from all classes of society. The most prominent of the victims were the Protestant bishops Latimer, Ridley, and Hooper and Archbishop Cranmer. Mary's persecutions won her the nickname "Bloody Mary." Many others, the Marian exiles, fled to the continent and settled as colonists in Geneva, Frankfurt am Main, Strasbourg, and elsewhere. On the continent they came more strongly under the growing influence of Calvinism. Mary died in 1558, her plans for a complete restoration of the pre-1529 religious establishment frustrated by the opposition of Parliament and the people of England.

THE ELIZABETHAN SETTLEMENT

Mary Tudor was followed by her 25-year-old half-sister Elizabeth I, daughter of Henry VIII and Anne Boleyn.

Elizabeth's primary concern in her domestic and foreign policies was national unity under a strong monarch. Theological considerations were secondary. Religious differences were for a time tolerated. The Marian exiles returned home. Calvinism came to be a growing influence. The new queen was not identified with any religious group, though she did like the vestments and drama of the Roman Catholic ritual. Yet she was naturally opposed to the papacy that had declared her illegitimate. Unlike her predecessor, Elizabeth moved cautiously, recognizing that the vast majority of the common people were still Roman Catholic but that the middle class and many prominent persons were Protestant in sympathy. She appointed moderate Protestants as officials. In order to secure a Protestant clergy, Parliament passed in 1559 an Act of Supremacy that revived many of the Reformation statutes of Henry VIII and Edward VI. This act, among others, gave the queen the title of the "only supreme governor of this realm . . . as well in all spiritual or ecclesiastical things or causes, as temporal," avoiding the more offensive term "Supreme Head of the Church." All clergy, judges, and high officials had to swear that they accepted the subordinate position of the church to the crown; those who refused to take the oath were deprived of their offices. The somewhat Zwinglian Second Prayer Book (1552) was slightly revised to include more Catholic passages and ambiguous phrases, and this Elizabethan Book of Common Prayer was to be followed by all. Absence from religious service was punishable by fine. Elizabeth insisted on the retention of certain Catholic usages, as the wearing of white surplices by the clergy and their being called "priests." The traditional role of the bishops in confirmation and ordination was carefully preserved.

So conservative and cautious was Elizabeth in her religious policy that the popes hesitated for a long time in denouncing her. In 1570, however, Pius V excommunicated the "Pretended Queen of England and those heretics adhering to her." The bull also declared that Englishmen did not owe obedience to her and the present laws of England because she had "forbidden the prelates, clergy and people to acknowledge the Church of Rome" and "the observance of the true religion."[5]

Central to the Elizabethan Settlement in religion are the moderate Thirty-nine Articles, enacted by Parliament in 1571. Showing less conservatism than Lutheranism and leaving room for individual interpretation, these articles have remained the authoritative statement of Anglican doctrine ever since. They recognize only two sacraments and define the Lord's Supper in a Calvinistic manner as "a parttakyng of the body of Christe, and likewyse the cuppe of blessing, is a parttakyng of the blood of Christe. Transubstantiation is repugnaunt to the playne wordes of scripture. The body of Christe is geuen, taken, and eaten in the Supper *only after an heauenly and spirituall maner*" (italics ours).[6] The articles enjoin infant baptism and adherence to the Apostles', Nicene, and Athanasian creeds. According to the articles, general councils are to be called only by order of the rulers, as in the early Christian centuries. All councils can err. Marriage of the clergy is permitted.

ANGLICAN RITES

The Anglican rite of Baptism was administered on the Sunday or holy day immediately following birth.[7] It was performed in English in the presence of the congregation, "that the congregation there present may testify the receiving of them that be newly Baptized into the number of Christ's Church, as also because in the Baptism of Infants every man present may be put in remembrance of his own profession made to God in his Baptism." The rite was held after the last lesson during the morning or evening prayer service. After prayers the godparents, on behalf of the infant, renounced the devil and all his works and professed belief in the articles of the Apostles' Creed. Baptism was performed in the name of the Trinity by dipping the child into the water, "so it be discreetly and warily done." If the child was weak, it was considered sufficient "to pour water upon it." Sprinkling did not become common in England until after 1600. Provisions were made for private baptism at home in cases of emergency. Besides water and the role of the sponsors, the only remnant of the traditional ceremony was the signing of the cross on the child's forehead immediately after immersion.

Baptized children were admitted to the rite of confirmation as soon as they could recite in English the articles of faith, the Lord's Prayer, and the Ten Commandments. They also had to be able to answer correctly such catechetical questions as the bishop or his appointee should ask them. Instruction in the faith was given by the parish priest, the curate or vicar, every Sunday and holy day for one-half hour. The priest then informed the bishop of the names of those who were ready for presentation by a godfather or godmother. The rite included prayers and the "imposition of hands" by the bishop. Confirmation was now a prerequisite for Communion.[8]

Holy Communion was envisioned as the normal Sunday service. The Eucharistic liturgy was stern, stately, and penitential in character and thus in marked contrast with the more joyous Mass of the Lutheran Reformation. Regulations required that every parishioner should receive Communion at least three times a year, of which Easter was to be one. After the reading of the collect and the traditional Scripture lessons, exhortations, and prayers, the minister made a general confession of sins before the kneeling congregation and pronounced a general absolution. The bread and the wine were distributed as the communicants knelt before the Communion table, which was covered with a "fair white linen cloth." The bread used in the sacrament was to be such "as is usual to be eaten at the Table with other meats, but the best and purest wheat bread, that conveniently may be gotten." The use of Eucharistic vestments was permitted, but they were generally replaced by the black cassock and simple white surplice. Any bread and wine that remained after the service was given to the curate of the parish for his own use.[9]

OPPOSITION TO THE SETTLEMENT

Many Englishmen were dissatisfied with the Elizabethan Settlement. The conservatives, while often antipapal for nationalist reasons, disapproved of the doctrinal changes. On the other hand, many Protestants thought that the settlement, basically a compromise for unity's sake, was too conservative and too close to Roman Catholicism. The returning Marian exiles, numbering over 500, especially attacked the settlement. These nonconforming Calvinists were called Puritans, for they wanted to "purify" the Anglican Church of the "vestiges of popery" that remained in ritual and in the episcopal church government. As opposition grew and as propapal plots aimed at deposing Elizabeth occurred, the government took stern action with stringent laws against treason, for religious and political convictions were inextricably intertwined. During the last 20 years of Elizabeth's reign, about 250 Roman Catholics were executed, chiefly for treason. As the Puritans grew in strength and as their literature became more abusive, Parliament passed the Act Against Seditious Sectaries (1593) for "the preventing and avoiding of such great inconveniences and perils as might happen and grow by the wicked and dangerous practices of seditious sectaries and disloyal persons."[10] Those over the age of 16 who did not attend services given according to the laws of England were to be imprisoned. Many fled to Holland. However, by the end of Elizabeth's rule in 1603, Roman Catholics and Puritans were still strong enough to cause difficulties for the Anglican government in the 17th century.

PROTESTANTISM COMES TO SCOTLAND

The Puritans found more sympathy for their views in the land to the north of England, for Calvinism had become firmly established in Scotland, then independent from the English. Here, too, there had been a long preparation for the advent of Protestantism. The moral and spiritual state of the clergy was worse in Scotland than elsewhere. Dissatisfaction with the wealthy hierarchy and dissolute clergy was strong among the independent-minded Scots, and Wycliffe's views had found sympathetic understanding. Despite official prohibition and suppression, Luther's works were widely read and his ideas preached. Protestantism found strong support among the barons, and religious differences became part of the struggle of the nobility against a combination of crown and hierarchy. King James V died in 1542, leaving his week-old daughter Mary Stuart as queen of Scots. There was a brief period during which Protestantism was favored by the regency, but the country soon came under the control of Cardinal David Beaton, who followed a pro-French and anti-English policy. The young Mary was sent to France to be raised by the Guises, a powerful and conservative Catholic family. The cardinal's repression of the growing Protestant and pro-English movement, especially his execution of the courageous preacher George Wishart, led to his own murder at St. Andrews in May 1546.

JOHN KNOX

The little band of armed conspirators, secure in the castle of St. Andrews, received as their chaplain a refugee priest named John Knox. This 32-year-old disciple of Wishart had at times protected his teacher with a two-handed sword, and now he became an implacable fighter for Calvinism. When the arrival of a French fleet forced the group in the castle to surrender, Knox and his companions were made galley slaves. Released early in 1549, Knox went to England and began his real work as a reformer under Edward VI. Again his work was interrupted, this time by the accession of Mary Tudor in 1554. Knox fled to Frankfurt and then went to Geneva, where he spent some time with Calvin; he also stayed with Bullinger at Zurich. After a short visit to England, where he married, and to Scotland, where he preached for nine months, Knox returned to Geneva, the "perfect school of Christ," to minister to other English-speaking refugees. During his absence a few Scottish noblemen, later called the Lords of the Congregation, formed in 1557 the first Scottish Covenant. In this covenant they committed their lives and fortunes "to establish and maintain the Word of God" in Scotland. In 1558 Mary Stuart married Francis, the dauphin who was soon to be king of France; in the same year Mary Tudor died and was succeeded by Elizabeth. The Marian refugees now returned to England, and Knox would have gone there also; but Elizabeth was offended by his violent political tract, *The First Blast of the Trumpet against the Monstrous Regiment of Women*, which Knox had directed against the governments of Mary Tudor and Mary of Guise, the wife of the former James V and then the regent of Scotland.

CALVINISM TRIUMPHS

Knox returned to his homeland, where he led the forces of Calvinism against the regent, who was attempting to repress the Reformation. All Europe awaited the outcome of this contest, for it was not an internal affair alone; it involved not only the future of Scotland but Protestant England and Roman Catholic France as well. European Protestantism hung in the balance, for Mary Stuart was now queen of France and threatened to tie Scotland to Catholic France and thus isolate Protestant England. However, the arrival of an English fleet and army led to the surrender of the French troops in Scotland. The regent, Mary of Guise, had died in June 1560. Emboldened by victory, the Scottish Parliament ratified in the same year the 25 articles of the Calvinist Confession of Faith prepared by Knox and his associates. They also cut Scotland's ties with Rome, annulled previous anti-Protestant acts, and condemned the Mass. A Book of Discipline was also prepared, and although it was not approved by Parliament, its proposals for the government of the Scottish church were accepted by the General Assembly of the church. This work provided a constitution and disciplinary rules for the Reformed Church of Scotland. The government of the church was organized on the principle of democratic assemblies, beginning with the parish church and extending upward through the synods to the General Assembly. Representative leadership in church government was developed through the elected and ordained elders, or presbyters. The endeavor was to follow the New Testament pattern of church government and worship. The Scottish church with its presbyterian system thus differed from the Anglican episcopal church with its bishops and more "Catholic" forms of worship. This difference was to be a source of conflict between the two nations in the 17th century. The principle of popular (representative) leadership in Scotland, however, meant that the church there had a much greater impact on the lives of the people. The English clergy, often drawn from the ranks of the younger sons of the nobility and not too well educated for the ministry, were also less popular and less respected than their Scottish counterparts.

The Reformed Church of Scotland had no sooner been established in 1560 than it was confronted by the return of the Catholic Mary Stuart in August 1561. Her husband, Francis II of France, had died in 1560 at the age of 16. Both Elizabeth of England and the Scots, most of whom were now Calvinists, feared that the French-educated queen would attempt to use force and the support of her Guise relatives in France to bring her land back to Catholicism and place it under the influence of France. In that country the wars between the crown and the Huguenots were beginning. However, the shrewd and self-confident young queen did not follow the advice of her counselors to use French troops to repress Protestantism in her realm. Instead, she tried persuasion and dissimulation and held a series of conferences with Knox and his colleagues. Nothing was accomplished by these means, for the fiery Knox could not be persuaded or intimidated. The General Assembly continued to meet without the permission of Mary. In 1567 Mary's husband, Lord Darnley, was murdered. The Queen then hastily married the unscrupulous Earl of Bothwell, but the Scottish nobles refused to allow him to become king. Instead, Mary was deposed and her infant son was crowned as James VI. Parliament declared that all future kings must swear to maintain Protestantism in Scotland. It also recognized the authority of the General Assembly of the Church of Scotland. Mary fled to England, where she was eventually executed for complicity in plots to overthrow Elizabeth.

THE REFORMATIONS IN ENGLAND AND SCOTLAND COMPARED

While both England and Scotland rejected Roman Catholicism, the reformations that resulted took different forms. The English Reformation was an act of state in which the monarch and Parliament held final authority in discipline and doctrine. The episcopal form of church government and more traditional forms of worship were retained. The Anglican Church was a compromise between the extremes of continental Protestantism and Roman Catholicism. The definition of the compromise took long to evolve. On the other hand, the Scottish Reformation was a more radical and quicker break with the past. The Scottish nobles, with the support of the people, brought into being a church firmly based on Calvinism, with a representative church government, independent of secular authorities, replacing the episcopal hierarchy. Scottish ministers were mostly sons of God-fearing and Bible-reading commoners and were highly respected for their learning. The Presbyterian church services, based on the Genevan services, became known for their austere simplicity and the singing of psalms and other Scripture in vernacular paraphrase. Both ministers and services were somewhat in contrast to what was the rule in the Church of England.

Notes and References

1. Hans J. Hillerbrand, *The Reformation: A Narrative History Related by Contemporary Observers and Participants* (New York and Evanston: Harper & Row, 1964), p. 332; Roland H. Bainton, *The Age of the Reformation*, Anvil Book 13 (New York: D. Van Nostrand Co., 1956), p. 143.
2. Hillerbrand, p. 339.
3. Bainton, *Age*, p. 145.
4. Ibid., p. 146.
5. F. E. Hutchinson, *Cranmer and the English Reformation* (New York: Collier Books, 1962), p. 117.
6. Bainton, *Age*, p. 159.
7. *Liturgies and Occasional Forms of Prayer set forth in the Reign of Queen Elizabeth*, ed. W. K. Clay (Cambridge: University Press, 1847), pp. 199 – 205.
8. Ibid., pp. 210 – 16.
9. Ibid., pp. 180 – 98.
10. Bainton, *Age*, p. 149.

CHAPTER 8

THE CATHOLIC
REFORMATION AND
COUNTER REFORMATION

PRELUDE

Long before the Protestant Reformation, there had been pious men and women in the Christian church who, either as individuals or by banding together with kindred spirits, had sought to reform the church from within. Even Luther, it must be remembered, had started out as a loyal son of the church with no intention of breaking with the church of his day. The authorities, however, had excommunicated the Reformer and placed him and his followers among the unorthodox. This brought about the separation. But there were many other reformers and reform movements that were never pushed beyond the established boundaries of orthodoxy, although at times they narrowly skirted the edge.

The mystics of the 14th and 15th centuries sought to reform the church by making their own lives models of piety, devotion, charity, and contemplation. There were other groups, including the Christian humanists, who long before Luther protested against the effects of secularism, wealth, and politics on the hierarchy and life of the whole church. The councils that had met during the first half of the 15th century had sought, with negligible results, to achieve reform. If all these reforming groups, and the councils especially, had been successful in achieving a viable reform in "head and members," Luther's name might never have been known beyond the circle of his family and friends.

REFORMS IN SPAIN

An effective Catholic Reformation began in Spain about the time Luther was born. The reform was led by Cardinal

Francisco Jiménez de Cisneros (d. 1517). His movement was devoted primarily toward an educational reform along humanistic lines. Erasmian Christian humanism was very influential among Spanish intellectuals; but with the spread of Protestantism, with its direct link with humanism, the works and ideals of Erasmus were condemned by the Inquisition. Prominent Spanish Erasmians in the early 16th century were Juan de Valdes and Juan de Vives. The other influential element in the Spanish reform was mysticism, and St. Teresa of Avila is the most noted figure.

NEW ITALIAN ORDERS

With the corruption and abuse so evident in troubled Italy, a vigorous Catholic Reformation arose there in the early 16th century. As in the Middle Ages, the reform movement was spearheaded by religious orders. About 1517 the Oratory of Divine Love was founded in Rome. Composed of both laity and clergy, many of them illustrious men, this order put new life into Italian Christianity through its members' devotions and charity among the poor. Affiliated groups sprang up throughout Italy. In 1524 papal sanction was given to the Theatines, an order of devout priests who combined preaching and works of charity in their parishes with a life governed by the requirements of a monastic rule. This order spread beyond the territories of Italy. Another group devoted to the restoration of piety and morality in Italy was the austere Capuchin order, a reformed Franciscan order.

THE JESUITS

While these orders did much good work in revitalizing Christian life in Italy and elsewhere, they were not intended or designed to fight Protestantism. This was to be the great task assigned to the Society of Jesus, or the Jesuits. The founder of this influential order was a Spanish nobleman, Ignatius of Loyola, who was born in 1491. His right leg was broken by a French cannonball during the defense of the city of Pamplona (1521), an injury that was to make him permanently lame. During the long period of recovery, his reading and meditation led him to renounce his old way of life and to resolve to become a soldier for Christ and the church. He then wrote the plan of his famous book, *Spiritual Exercises*, which, when completed, reflected his own religious experiences. This handbook offered detailed instructions through which the reader would develop inner peace, self-control, and discipline and finally surrender his will and being to God and the church (see Appendix, No. 7). Thus, thoroughly disciplined by meditations and spiritual exercises, the man was ready to submit himself completely to the church: "To arrive at the truth in all things, we ought always to be ready to believe that what seems to us white is black, if the hierarchical Church so defines it."[1]

Ignatius' desire to convert the Muslims in Palestine was frustrated by the Franciscans there. He thereupon decided to prepare himself for his missionary task by acquiring a better education. At the universities of Alcalá and Salamanca he ran into trouble with the Inquisition because of his unauthorized preaching activities. In 1528 Ignatius entered the College of Montaigu in Paris, a college that John Calvin had just left. By the time Ignatius left Paris in 1535, this small (5 feet 2 inches), deformed, but enthusiastic man had attracted nine faithful disciples, including Francis Xavier, Diego Laynez, and Alfonso Salmeron. Unable to go to Palestine because of war, the group went to Rome to offer their services to the pope. In 1540 papal approval was gained for their new order from Paul III. In the papal bull the Society of Jesus is said to have been "founded for the special purpose of providing spiritual consolation for the furtherance of souls in Christian living and doctrine, the propagation of faith by public preaching, and the ministry of the Word of God, spiritual exercises and deeds of mercy, and above all the instruction of the ignorant in the Christian religion and by hearing the confession of Christian believers."[2]

Besides the usual monastic vows, the constitution of the new order called for a special vow of complete obedience to the pope: "If then the present Pope or his successors should send us for the improvement of souls or the propagation of the faith to the Turks or other infidels even in India or to heretics, schismatics or some of the faithful, we are to obey without evasion or excuse."[3] The Jesuits, as they came to be called, practiced only moderate asceticism, for nothing was to interfere with their efficiency. Instead of establishing religious communities like the monastic orders, the Jesuits became very active in the affairs of the world. The upper classes, not the masses, were the object of their efforts and attention. The military character of the organization, the discipline, and the subordination of the individual's will to that of his superior all contributed to the achievement of the society's goals.

Under the skillful generalship of Ignatius, trained Jesuits were sent throughout Europe and made a valiant effort to retain Roman Catholics in the church, to stir up new life and zeal in it, and to bring those already separated back into the fold. They won approval of the rulers by their tact, manners, absolute devotion, self-denial, resourcefulness, and learning. Popular as confessors to rulers and men of high influence, they did not hesitate to use their influence in matters of state. In existing universities and in their own excellent schools and colleges, they trained the youth so thoroughly in Roman Catholicism that that faith was, as a rule, forever retained by their students. The order soon grew in size, power, and wealth. As obedient shock troops of the papacy, they were sent from one danger area to another. As zealous crusaders for the church, and with the powerful support of the Hapsburg rulers, they recovered much territory from Protestantism in southern Germany and in Austria, Hungary, Bohemia, and Poland. In North and South America, Jesuits explored the wilderness and made converts among Indians. Francis Xavier spent 11 years in India and the Far East converting Muslims, Hindus, and Buddhists. No single force proved so advantageous to the Roman Catholic Church in revitalizing its own ranks and in turning the tide of Protestantism as did the Society of Jesus.

REFORM OF THE PAPACY

The popes gradually assumed a position of leadership in the Catholic Reformation. It was a slow and painful process, for no matter how much disposed toward reform a pope personally might be, he had to overcome the massive resistance of members of the Curia, the cardinals, and other prelates who profited from the rampant corruption. The Renaissance popes, Leo X (1513–21), Adrian VI, and Clement VII (1523–34), either were tolerant of abuses or could not overcome the dead weight of the entrenched corruption and abuse.

With the aged Paul III (1534–49) the Catholic Reformation gradually showed a new spirit and entered into what might be called the Counter (Protestant) Reformation stage. Paul III was a paradoxical figure. In his personal life the pope was notoriously immoral. Frank in his nepotism, he elevated two of his nephews to the cardinalate at the ages of 14 and 16. On the other hand, confronted by a vigorous and spreading Protestantism that was feeding on the people's discontent with the corruption and abuses in the church, Paul III appointed a commission of nine cardinals to consider the matter of reform and present a plan for action. Their *Consilium (Advice)* was presented in 1538. In no uncertain terms this remarkable document condemned, among others, papal absolutism, simony, the ordination of incompetent and immoral youths, abuses in the bestowal of benefices and bishoprics, pluralities, nonresident bishops, neglect of duties by the cardinals, the teaching of impiety at the universities, evils in monasticism, and the deceptions practiced on the simple folk.[4] The clandestine publication of this report was hailed by the Protestants as completely supporting the charges of Luther and the other reformers. So strong and candid were its denunciations, the report was later placed on the Index of Prohibited Books, a catalog of books that Roman Catholics were forbidden to read.

THE ROMAN INQUISITION

After the failure of an attempt to reconcile Protestantism and Roman Catholicism at a conference at Ratisbonn in 1541, the new spirit of reform led Paul III to establish in 1542 the Roman Inquisition. This was based on the model of the notorious but efficient Spanish Inquisition. Six cardinals, led by the rigid and zealous Giovanni Caraffa, were named Inquisitors General with wide jurisdiction "to investigate by way of inquisition [inquiry] all and single who wander from the way of the Lord and the Catholic faith, as well as those suspected of heresy, together with their followers and abettors, public or private, direct or indirect. The guilty and the suspects are to be imprisoned and proceeded against up to the final sentence." [5] The Inquisition moved against the lowly and those in high offices, including several cardinals. Many Italians with leanings toward Protestantism fled, and the evangelical movement was all but eliminated in Italy. Although it was originally intended that the Roman Inquisition should function throughout Roman Catholic Europe, such widespread activity was dependent on the support of the secular powers. This support was not forthcoming, and the Roman Inquisition was limited to Italy.

THE COUNCIL OF TRENT

Luther, Charles V, and many others had repeatedly called for a general council to decide the religious issues that were splitting Europe. The agitation increased as reluctant popes toyed with the idea. The popes remembered only too well the attacks on papal absolutism in the period of conciliarism. The recurring wars and political maneuvering also produced delays. Yielding to pressure, Paul III finally issued a call for a general council to meet at Mantua in May 1537, but he was forced by war to postpone the sessions. The same pope then called for a council to meet on Nov. 1, 1542, at Trent, a city in Austria just across the border from the Italian state of Venice. Again war between Charles V and Francis I forced a postponement until Dec. 13, 1545, when the Council of Trent formally opened. The Protestants refused to send delegates. The 25 sessions of this important council were held in three periods: 1545–47, 1551–52, and 1562–63.

From the very beginning the council's deliberations were characterized by very spotty and even poor representation, court intrigues, vigorous and often acrimonious debate, bickering, and inner struggles between the popes and the secular rulers and between the bishops and the papal party. Dogma and reform were discussed concurrently, a compromise solution to the emperor's demand for reform and the pope's desire for a definition of dogma. Since the papal legates presided over the sessions of the council, and since Italian prelates always outnumbered those from other countries, papal control of the council was assured. As the council's purpose and prevailing mood were defensive in the face of the Protestant revolt, the decrees tended to be conservative and defensive instead of forward looking and conciliatory.

In doctrinal matters the council placed Scripture and tradition on an equal basis as opposed to the Protestant acceptance of the primacy of the Bible. To the chagrin of many of the humanistically trained theologians, Jerome's ancient Vulgate edition of the Bible was declared the authoritative text of the Scriptures, which only the church could interpret. The Protestant view that man, depraved by original sin, could perform no meritorious work of himself but was dependent on grace alone, was rejected after heated debate by the council, which also denied justification by faith alone. Both faith and good works were declared necessary for justification. The seven sacraments and the doctrine of transubstantiation were upheld. The council reaffirmed all things rejected by the Protestants: purgatory, invocation of saints, celibacy, papal power, the Mass as a propitiatory sacrifice, and Communion under one element. Thus, in doctrinal matters, the decrees of the Council of Trent were very conservative, strongly anti-Protestant, and gave little evidence of having been affected by the theological debates of the previous decades.

In matters of discipline and reform, the council's membership was often divided, but the need for reform was neither denied nor underestimated. Primarily, the reform decrees centered on the role of the bishop in his diocese. Pluralism and neglect were condemned, and religious instruction, preaching, and visitation were enjoined. Other decrees called for reform in the lives of all clergy, with moderation, simplicity, industry, morality, and frugality prescribed.

Concubinage was forbidden. In order that better qualified clergy might be obtained, theological seminaries were to be established in every diocese, and the clergy were to be examined before ordination or appointment. Periodic synods, or meetings of the clergy, were ordered. The office of the indulgence seller, but not indulgences themselves, was eliminated. Superstitious devotional practices were curbed and liturgical practices made uniform. The preaching activities of the monastic clergy were restricted and the administration of these orders tightened. In all, a comprehensive program of reform was promulgated — a century too late.

The Council of Trent was an important landmark in the history of Christianity. The dogmas and practices of Roman Catholicism were so carefully defined that only a few additions have been made in the succeeding centuries. This meant the introduction of a certain rigidity; the variations that had been permitted before the Protestant Reformation were now denied. The understanding of justification and of the relation of Scripture and tradition, for instance, had not been officially defined before. The Inquisition now had the criteria for orthodoxy with which to test the views of those suspected of heresy. Far from achieving a basis for unity and reconciliation within Christendom, the decrees of the Council of Trent made such a hope more unlikely. By defining dogma, removing abuse and corruption, and strengthening the central authority of the popes, the Roman Catholic Church was enabled to present a united and firm front in its defensive and counter measures against Protestantism.

THE INDEX

The repressive spirit that emanated from the decisions of the Council of Trent can best be seen in the Index of Prohibited Books which the council ordered prepared. Censorship and destruction of unorthodox books had long been exercised within Christianity, but the advent of printing (ca. 1450) and the resultant flood of books made censorship a great problem. In 1557 the Roman Inquisition published a long list of books to be burned, and two years later Pope Paul IV issued the first *Index librorum prohibitorum* (Index of Prohibited Books). The Council of Trent appointed a commission to prepare a more comprehensive and stricter index. This Tridentine Index, or Index of Pope Pius IV, appeared in 1564 and condemned works under 10 general rules. A commission, the Congregation of the Index, was established in 1571 to revise and publish new editions in the attempt to discourage Roman Catholics from reading works thought detrimental to faith and morals. Just what effect the Index in its various editions has had on thought and literature is difficult to assess, but many have condemned it for creating intolerance and repressing the flow of ideas. In 1966 the Index was declared discontinued.

A STRENGTHENED ROMAN CATHOLIC CHURCH

By means of reformed and reforming popes, the creation of new and active religious orders, the work of the Roman Inquisition, and by the dogmatic and disciplinary decisions of the Council of Trent, a new and greatly strengthened Roman Catholic Church emerged in the last quarter of the 16th century. It was in a much more favorable position than before to combat the non-Roman-Catholic part of a divided Christendom. The authority of the papacy was firmly established over the church's administration, and under papal leadership the worst abuses and corruption were corrected. Nepotism and simony were ended, the indulgence seller disappeared, and the confessional box was introduced, with a screen separating the confessor and the priest, in an effort to prevent dangers resulting from confessional intimacy. The institutions within the Roman Church and the personnel of these organizations took on a new life. In its encounter with the Reformation, Catholicism came to grips with basic issues and showed little tendency to change the traditional interpretations and practice. Indeed, the preservation of a conservative orthodoxy was guaranteed by placing the right of interpretation of Scriptures and tradition in the hands of the pope. Yet new vitality and spirituality were engendered everywhere, and the new forces in Catholicism were able to stop and even roll back the advancing tide of Protestantism. At the same time the definitive statements on Roman Catholic doctrine meant an increase in tensions and animosities between the now clearly divided elements in Christendom.

Notes and References

1. Edward McNall Burnes, *The Counter Reformation* (Princeton: D. Van Nostrand Co., 1964), p. 127.
2. Hans J. Hillerbrand, *The Reformation: A Narrative History Related by Contemporary Observers and Participants* (New York and Evanston: Harper & Row, 1964), pp. 437 – 38.
3. Roland H. Bainton, *The Age of the Reformation,* Anvil Book 13 (New York: D. Van Nostrand Co., 1956), p. 154.
4. Ibid., p. 153.
5. Ibid., p. 155.

CHAPTER 9

EPILOG

In the three centuries following A. D. 1300, the Christian church was dramatically changed. By the beginning of the 17th century, Orthodox Christianity of the eastern Mediterranean area and in the Balkans had long been under the control of the Muslim Turks with the patriarch of Constantinople a subject of the sultan. In the West the unity that had characterized the late medieval church was shattered for all time. The West was now divided into two opposing religious camps — Roman Catholic and Protestant. Roman Catholicism was predominant in the Italian states, Spain, Austria, France, Portugal, Ireland, Hungary, Poland, Southern Germany, and the Spanish Lowlands. Various forms of Protestantism, often hostile to one another, held ascendancy in Bohemia, northern Germany, the Scandinavian countries, the United Provinces, some of the Swiss cantons, England, and Scotland. Strong Protestant minorities could be found in Austria, Poland, Hungary, and France.

ROMAN CATHOLICISM, 1600

In addition to being reduced in number of adherents, the Roman Catholic Church in 1600 differed markedly in character from its parental, late medieval institution. The pope, to be sure, still held the same position of authority in the church as in the 14th century. However, the exercise of his spiritual authority was somewhat restricted by a strengthened episcopacy. His political power was very much limited by the powerful rulers of the new national states, a number of whom were now Protestant. Papal claims of universal dominance were no longer recognized except in

the interpretation of doctrine. Even that claim was acceptable only to Roman Catholics. The Roman Catholic clergy
was much revitalized by the forces of the Catholic Counter
Reformation and by the confrontation with Protestantism.
The new orders, especially the Jesuits, had deepened and
reformed the religious life of Catholicism, while the canons
and decrees of the Council of Trent had established firm
discipline and had clearly defined the criteria of orthodoxy.
The most obvious abuses and corruption within the hierarchy
had been corrected. Monasticism had become, in general,
less ascetic and more activist in missions.

PROTESTANTISM, A. D. 1600

By the end of the 16th century, Protestantism had
developed a variety of forms of which Lutheranism, Calvinism, Anabaptism, and Anglicanism were the most easily
distinguished. Once the principle of the priesthood of all
believers and the right of individual interpretation of Scripture are accepted, an infinite variety of religious expressions
and ecclesiastical organizations is possible. The continuous
development of Protestant sects during and after the Reformation was the result. The 17th and 18th centuries, for
example, were to see the rise of Quakers, Methodists, Congregationalists, and Baptists — to name some of the more
prominent. But within the diversity of Protestantism in the
16th century, there was unity in certain basic areas. All
Protestants rejected the papacy, the requirement of clerical
celibacy, purgatory, monasticism, salvation through faith
and good works, the majority of the medieval sacraments,
and many other facets of traditional Christianity which
they felt were medieval additions not based on Scripture.
All Protestants professed to build their doctrines only on
the rediscovered Bible.

LITURGICAL CHANGES

Since profound differences existed between Roman
Catholic and Protestant dogma, and to some extent within
Protestantism itself, they were reflected in the rites and

liturgies of the churches. Except for some minor changes made by the Council of Trent, mainly in the interest of uniformity, the Roman Catholic rites and ceremonies remained within the late medieval tradition. Protestant rites followed the simplified patterns laid down by the various Reformers. As usual, Lutheranism and Anglicanism were more conservative in this respect than the Reformed and Radical groups.

THE PROTESTANT MINISTRY

It was not only in doctrine and liturgy that the Protestantism of 1600 differed markedly from Roman Catholicism. Protestantism also produced a new and characteristic leadership for the church—the Protestant ministry. Nowhere within Protestantism was the clergy considered a separate and special spiritual caste, as in Catholicism. The Protestant minister was simply one who for the sake of public order was appointed to certain duties which in principle every Christian was entitled to perform. Those pastors with better education and training became the influential ministers of churches in towns and courts; the poorer-trained clergy found positions in the country parishes. As most of the Protestant ministers were poorly paid, there did not develop those differences in social position and wealth that were often found in the Roman Catholic hierarchy.

The social status of the Protestant minister was also sharply distinguished from his Roman Catholic counterpart in that more often than not he was married and the head of a family. He thus actively demonstrated that God was best served in an ordinary and common social setting. All of the Reformers married, and a married clergy became traditional in Protestantism, with the pastor's wife playing an important role in the life and work of the ministry.

Another distinguishing mark of Protestantism was its preaching. Numerous services were conducted each week in all Protestant churches, and the instructional sermon, delivered in the vernacular, was the primary feature of most of these. Of the great reformers, Luther was undoubtedly the most popular preacher. He spoke well, skillfully and simply expounding the Bible with the aid of his own vivid imagination and keen observation of men. His delivery was marked by the use of proverbs and the vocabulary of the common people. He also knew when to stop. Zwingli was too intellectual in his sermons; Calvin, too impersonal. The growth of a preaching ministry in Protestantism was slow at first as many of the early preachers had been priests, not trained for preaching, or they were often uneducated and inexperienced. Later in the 16th century the Protestant universities produced a clergy better educated in the Bible, but the skill and art of preaching was not taught.

EDUCATION

It was natural that both the Protestant Reformation and the Roman Catholic reform movements should influence education in the 16th and later centuries. Every religious group soon came to realize the importance of schools at all levels for religious training and to assure permanence for the work of reform. The influence of the Protestant reformers was especially seen in the spread of education to larger numbers of children and adults. Luther had urged that all the communities of Germany should establish public schools with compulsory attendance for both boys and girls. Only in this way could a laity be developed fit for their calling from God in the world and in the church. Luther also advocated the teaching of vocational skills. Melanchthon was called "The Teacher of Germany" because of his help in establishing schools in 56 towns and because of the widely used textbooks he wrote. The *Ecclesiastical Ordinances* of Geneva had set forth the need "to prepare youth for the ministry and civil government." Both Luther and Calvin wanted a close association between church and state in moral and religious instruction. Certain of the new Catholic orders were noted for their teaching at the elementary level. With the notable exception of the later Jesuit schools, the aristocratic approach of Renaissance education was abandoned, and the new schools founded by all the religious groups were democratic, open to all classes.

The advent of the Reformation, with its attendant strife

and confusion, initially had a detrimental effect on the universities of Europe. All the universities experienced a drastic decline in enrollment in the years that followed 1520. The University of Wittenberg recovered by 1540. In 1527 another Lutheran university was founded at Marburg. Other important Protestant universities were those at Zurich, Geneva, Leiden, Koenigsberg, Jena, Heidelberg, Cambridge, St. Andrews, and Edinburgh. New Catholic institutions of higher learning were established in Spain and Italy. In all universities, usually only those students were admitted whose faith matched the religion of the controlling church. There was a definite tendency in the 16th century for the universities to come under the authority of the local ruler. Conservatism marked the methods and the humanistic curricula of most institutions. Freedom of thought and expression by the faculty was restricted, and conformity to the prescribed religious pattern was imposed. The great scientific advances of the period were made independent of the university setting.

TOLERATION

The Reformation era was not an age of religious toleration. Protestants as well as Roman Catholics persecuted and even executed those whom they considered heretics and blasphemers. While Roman Catholic authorities relied on canon law and the decrees of the Council of Trent, Protestants used the Bible as the guide for their persecutions. The resuscitated ancient Roman law was the basis for the repudiation and persecution of anti-Trinitarians and Anabaptists. Calvin burned Servetus, but banishment was the more usual punishment in Protestant lands. However, despite the intolerance, forces were at work in the 16th century that were eventually to lead to religious liberty. The very existence of so many rival factions often meant that no one group was strong enough to force its will on the rest. But only in later centuries did the idea develop that variance in religious views neither weakened the unity of the state nor lead to the corruption of society.

DEMOCRACY

Democracy, the system of government in which all the citizens of a state participate in matters of local or national policy and in which these citizens have equal and inalienable rights, is a fairly modern development. The democracy of today is the result of a long and slow growth that goes back to Old Testament times. From the Hebrews and from early Christianity came the concepts of the dignity of each human being, the equality of all men before God, and the right and duty to disobey and criticize unjust rulers. But the principles of democracy were seldom evident in the ecclesiastical and feudal civilization of the Middle Ages.

While political and even social democracy are not at all characteristic of the 16th century, Protestantism did give impetus to the growth of democracy. Luther's concept of the priesthood of all believers was an attack on the authoritarian hierarchical system and encouraged individual responsibility and freedom of decision. Calvinism originated in republican Geneva and soon was in open opposition to tyrannical forms of government everywhere, linked as these were to the forces opposing the Reformation. Calvinism also emphasized the rule of law, both Biblical and constitutional. The Anabaptists suffered terrible persecutions because of their passion for freedom of faith and thought. They and the Bohemian Brethren alone demanded the separation of church and state, but their views gained no widespread support.

THE ARTS

Of all the arts, music was most influenced by the reform movements of the 16th century. Zwingli, although himself a musician, abolished music from the church service. However, by the late 16th century, congregational singing had been reintroduced at Zurich. Luther loved music, including polyphony, and was himself an able musician. Under his influence, there developed the great Lutheran chorales that enhanced the service. The greater part of the liturgy was also sung by the congregation, and the Lutheran Church became "the singing church." Calvin restricted church music somewhat, but he recognized that "if the singing be tempered to that gravity which is fitting in the sight of God and the angels, it both lends dignity and grace to sacred actions and has the greatest value in kindling our hearts to a true zeal and eagerness to pray" (*Institutes* III. xx. 32). Calvinistic psalm-singing reached great heights of beauty and solemnity. The Anglican Church also produced considerable church music, although the English hymn is a later development. The Roman Catholic Church continued its use of trained choirs to sing the Latin music of the high Mass.

The content of visual arts embodies the life and thoughts of the people and artists who create it. The changes in economy, political life, and religion in the period under consideration naturally were reflected in architecture, painting, and sculpture. The Gothic art of the high Middle Ages had given way to the revival of classical forms of ancient Greece and Rome, reflecting the full life of the Renaissance individual and the secular spirit of the age. St. Peter's Basilica in Rome is an outstanding example of Renaissance ecclesiastical building. When the Reformation began in the 16th century, Renaissance art forms were already declining in grandeur because of excessive ornamentation and lavish decoration.

While many of the great Gothic churches in predominantly Protestant lands came to house reformed services, the new liturgical concepts usually demanded a different type of building. To Roman Catholics, the church building was truly the house of God with the divine presence direct and tangible in the consecrated elements of the Eucharist and in the signs and symbols of the sacramental mysteries. The focus of the building was therefore the altar. To the Protestants, the church was more of a meeting place for the congregation and for instruction in the Word of God during the services. The pulpit and lectern thus received a place of equal prominence with the Communion table or altar. Where iconoclasm prevailed, as in the Calvinistic Reformed Church, there was frequently an excessive plainness and lack of artistry in the churches. Lutheranism and Anglicanism retained the use of sculptured and painted objects as long as they were conducive to evangelical faith and not the subjects of superstitious veneration.

CONCLUSION

By 1600 the unity that had existed in the Western Christian church of 1300 had been disrupted. The new diversity led to mutual suspicion and the attempt to use arms to resolve religious differences. Although largely political in nature, both the Thirty Years' War in Germany (1618 – 48) and the Civil War in England (1642 – 60) arose out of religious tensions.

While the disunity in Christendom brought about by the Protestant Reformation is often deplored, the break in the external structure of the Christian church in the West was accompanied by an internal revitalization of the spirit. Out of the upheaval of the 16th century came a strengthening of religious life in the various components of Christianity. The worst abuses and the widespread corruption that had characterized the lax church of the Renaissance were eliminated, and a more vigorous discipline was instituted within the many branches of the church.

APPENDIX

READINGS FROM PRIMARY SOURCES

A number of primary sources for the period of the Renaissance and Reformation are conveniently available in the following paperback collections: *The Renaissance and the Reformation, 1300–1600,* ed. Donald Weinstein (New York: Free Press, 1965); *Renaissance and Reformation, 1300–1648,* ed. G. R. Elton (New York: Macmillan Co., 1963); *The Protestant Reformation,* ed. Hans J. Hillerbrand (New York: Harper & Row, 1968); *The Protestant Reformation,* ed. Lewis W. Spitz, Spectrum Book 140 (Englewood Cliffs, N. J.: Prentice-Hall, 1966); and *Martin Luther: Selections from His Writings,* ed. John Dillenberger, Anchor Book 271 (Garden City, N. Y.: Doubleday & Co., 1961).

NO. 1 MYSTICISM

In the mystical tradition the Imitation of Christ, *by Thomas a Kempis (d. 1471), is rightly considered one of the greatest devotional booklets of all times. It illustrates well the spirit of mysticism and the desire to reform the lives of individual Christians by a union of the soul with God.*

Book IV, Chapter 16: O most sweet and loving Lord, whom now I devoutly desire to receive, Thou knowest my infirmity and the necessity which I suffer, in what evils and vices I lie; how often I am weighed down, tempted, disturbed, and defiled. I come unto Thee for remedy, I beseech of Thee consolation and support. I speak unto Thee who knowest all things, to whom all my secrets are open, and who alone art able perfectly to comfort and help me. Thou knowest what good thing I most stand in need of, and how poor I am in virtues.

Behold, I stand poor and naked before Thee, requiring grace and imploring mercy. Refresh the hungry suppliant, kindle my coldness with the fire of Thy love, illuminate my blindness with the brightness of Thy presence. Turn thou all earthly things into bitterness for me, all grievous and contrary things into patience, all things worthless and created into contempt and oblivion. Lift up my heart unto Thee in Heaven, and suffer me not to wander over the earth. Be Thou alone sweet unto me from this day forward for ever, because Thou alone art my meat and drink, my love and joy, my sweetness and my whole good.

Oh that Thou wouldst altogether by Thy presence, kindle, consume, and transform me into Thyself; that I may be made one spirit with Thee, by the grace of inward union, and the melting of earnest love! Suffer me not to go away from Thee hungry and dry; but deal mercifully with me, as oftentimes Thou hast dealt wondrously with Thy saints. What marvel if I should be wholly kindled from Thee, and in myself should utterly fail, since Thou art fire always burning and never failing, love purifying the heart and enlightening the understanding.

Translation by William Benham, from *The Harvard Classics*, ed. C. W. Eliot, VII (New York: P. F. Collier & Sons, 1909), 375–76.

NO. 2 ANTICLERICALISM

While many writers wrote critical works on contemporary society and especially the clergy, The Praise of Folly, *by Desiderius Erasmus, was outstanding for its satire and wit. In these selections it must be remembered that Folly is speaking of her followers, the foolish ones.*

Then what shall I say of the people who so happily fool themselves with forged pardons for sins, measuring out time to be spent in purgatory as if with an hour-glass, and figuring its centuries, years, months, days, and hours as if from a mathematical table, beyond possibility of error? Or I might speak of those who will promise themselves any and every thing, relying upon certain charms or prayers devised by some pious imposter either for his soul's sake or for money, to bring them wealth, reputation, pleasure, plenty, good health, long life, and a green old age, and at last a seat next to Christ's in heaven — but they do not wish to get it too soon . . . .

I fancy that I see some merchant or soldier or judge laying down one small coin from his extensive booty and expecting that the whole cesspool of his life will be at once purified. He conceives that just so many perjuries, so many lustful acts, so many debauches, so many fights, murders, frauds, lies and so many breaches of faith, are bought off as by contract; and so bought off that with a clean slate he may start from scratch upon a new round of sins . . . . And is it not almost as bad when the several countries each lay claim to a particular saint of their own, and then assign particular powers respectively to the various saints and observe for each one his own peculiar rites of worship? One saint assists in time of toothache, another is propitious to women in travail, another recovers stolen goods, a fourth stands by with help in a shipwreck, and still another keeps the sheep in good repair; and so of the rest, though it would take too long to specify all of them. Some of them are good for a number of purposes, particularly the Virgin Mother, to whom the common people tend to attribute more than to the Son.

Coming nearest to these [the Theologians] in felicity are the men who generally call themselves "the religious" and "monks" — utterly false names both, since most of them keep as far away as they can from religion and no people are more in evidence in every sort of place. But I do not see how anything could be more dismal than these monks if I [Folly] did not succor them in many ways. For though people as a whole so detest this race of men that meeting one by accident is supposed to be bad luck, yet they flatter themselves to the queen's taste. For one thing, they reckon it the highest degree of piety to have no contact with literature, and hence they see to it that they do not know how to read. For another, when with asinine voices they bray out in church those psalms they have learned, by rote rather than by heart, they are convinced that they are anointing God's ears with the blandest

of oil. Some of them make a good profit from their dirtiness
and mendicancy, collecting their food from door to door
with importunate bellowing; nay, there is not an inn, public
conveyance, or ship where they do not intrude, to the great
disadvantage of the other common beggars. Yet according
to their account by their very dirtiness, ignorance, want of
manners, and insolence, these delightful fellows are representing to us the lives of the apostles . . . .

Our popes, cardinals, and bishops for some time now
have earnestly copied the state and practice of princes, and
come near to beating them at their own game. Let a bishop but
consider what his alb, the white emblem of sincerity, should
teach him, namely, a life in every way blameless; and what is
signified on his part by the two-horned miter, the two peaks
bound by the same knot—I suppose it is a perfect knowledge
of the Old and New Testaments; what is meant by covering
his hands with gloves, a clean administration of the sacrament
and one unsullied by any taint of human concerns; what the
crozier symbolizes, most watchful care of the flock put under
his charge; what is indicated by the cross that is carried before
him, to wit, a victory over all carnal affections. If he would
contemplate these and other lessons of the sort, I say, would
he not lead a sad and troubled life? But as it is, they do well
enough by way of feeding themselves; as for the other, the
care of the sheep, they delegate that to Christ himself, or else
refer it to their suffragans, as they call them, or other depu-
ties, Nor do they keep in mind the name they bear, or what
the word "bishop" means—labor, vigilance, solicitude. Yet in
raking in moneys they truly play the bishop, overseeing everything—and overlooking nothing.

In a similar way the cardinals, if they considered the
fact that they have succeeded to the places of the apostles,
would see that the same works are required of them as were
performed by their predecessors; that they are not lords,
but stewards, of spiritual things, and that shortly they are to
render an exact account of what they hold in trust . . . .

As to these Supreme Pontiffs who take the place of Christ,
if they tried to emulate His life, I mean His poverty, labors,
teaching, cross, and contempt for safety, if even they thought
upon the title of Pope—that is, Father—or the addition

"Most Holy," who on earth would be more afflicted? Who would purchase that seat at the price of every resource and effort? Or who defend it, when purchased, by the sword, by poison, or by anything else? Were wisdom to descend upon them, how it would inconvenience them! Wisdom, did I say? Nay, even a grain of salt would do it — a grain of that salt which is spoken of by Christ. It would lose them all that wealth and honor, all those possessions, triumphal progresses, office, dispensations, tributes, and indulgences; it would lose them so many horses, mules, and retainers; so many pleasures . . . .

The Praise of Folly, trans. from the Latin, with an essay and commentary, by Hoyt Hopewell Hudson (Princeton: Princeton University Press, 1941), pp. 56 – 98, passim.

NO. 3 THE NEW THEOLOGY

The spirit and content of Luther's new theology is present in The Freedom of a Christian, *which he wrote in 1520. Here the essentials of the Reformation phrase "justification by grace through faith" are eloquently expressed. While the Christian, through faith, is freed from a reliance on works, he is obligated to discipline himself and make his faith active in love, serving his neighbor.*

THE FREEDOM OF A CHRISTIAN

Many people have considered Christian faith an easy thing, and not a few have given it a place among the virtues. They do this because they have not experienced it and have never tasted the great strength there is in faith. It is impossible to write well about it or to understand what has been written about it unless one has at one time or another experienced the courage which faith gives a man when trials oppress him. But he who has had even a faint taste of it can never write, speak, meditate, or hear enough concerning it. . . .

To make the way smoother for the unlearned — for only them do I serve — I shall set down the following two propositions concerning the freedom and the bondage of the spirit:

A Christian is a perfectly free lord of all, subject to none.
A Christian is a perfectly dutiful servant of all, subject
to all.

These two theses seem to contradict each other. If,
however, they should be found to fit together they would
serve our purpose beautifully. . . . Love by its very nature
is ready to serve and be subject to him who is loved. . . .

Let us start, however, with something more remote from
our subject, but more obvious. Man has a twofold nature,
a spiritual and a bodily one. According to the spiritual nature,
which men refer to as the soul, he is called a spiritual, inner,
or new man. According to the bodily nature, which men refer
to as flesh, he is called a carnal, outward, or old man . . . .

One thing, and only one thing, is necessary for Christian
life, righteousness, and freedom. That one thing is the most
holy Word of God, the gospel of Christ . . . . Let us then
consider it certain and firmly established that the soul can
do without anything except the Word of God and that where
the Word of God is missing there is no help at all for the soul.
If it has the Word of God it is rich and lacks nothing since
it is the Word of life, truth, light, peace, righteousness,
salvation, joy, liberty, wisdom, power, grace, glory, and of
every incalculable blessing. . . . The Word is the gospel of
God concerning his Son, who was made flesh, suffered, rose
from the dead, and was glorified through the Spirit who
sanctifies. To preach Christ means to feed the soul, make it
righteous, set it free, and save it, provided it believes the
preaching. Faith alone is the saving and efficacious use of
the Word of God . . . . The Word of God cannot be received
and cherished by any works whatever but only by faith.
Therefore it is clear that, as the soul needs only the Word of
God for its life and righteousness, so it is justified by faith
alone and not any works; for if it could be justified by anything else, it would not need the Word, and consequently
it would not need faith. . . .

Now when a man has learned through the commandments to recognize his helplessness and is distressed about
how he might satisfy the law—since the law must be fulfilled
so that not a jot or tittle shall be lost, otherwise man will
be condemned without hope—then, being truly humbled and

reduced to nothing in his own eyes, he finds in himself nothing whereby he may be justified and saved. Here the second part of Scripture comes to our aid, namely, the promises of God which declare the glory of God . . . . That which is impossible for you to accomplish by trying to fulfil all the works of the law—many and useless as they all are—you will accomplish quickly and easily through faith. God our Father has made all things depend on faith so that whoever has faith will have everything, and whoever does not have faith will have nothing. . . .

From what has been said it is easy to see from what source faith derives such great power and why a good work or all good works together cannot equal it. No good work can rely upon the Word of God or live in the soul, for faith alone and the Word of God rule in the soul. Just as the heated iron glows like fire because of the union of fire with it, so the Word imparts its qualities to the soul. It is clear, then, that a Christian, has all that he needs in faith and needs no works to justify him; and if he has no need of works, he has no need of the law; and if he has no need of the law, surely he is free from the law. . . .

Not only are we the freest of kings, we are also priests forever, which is far more excellent than being kings, for as priests we are worthy to appear before God to pray for others and to teach one another divine things. These are the functions of priests, and they cannot be granted to any unbeliever. . . .

Now let us turn to the second part, the outer man. Here we shall answer all those who, offended by the word "faith" and by all that has been said, now ask, "If faith does all things and is alone sufficient unto righteousness, why then are good works commanded? We will take our ease and do no works and be content with faith." I answer: not so, you wicked men, not so. That would indeed be proper if we were wholly inner and perfectly spiritual men. But such we shall be only at the last day, the day of the resurrection of the dead. As long as we live in the flesh we only begin to make some progress in that which shall be perfected in the future life. . . . This is the place to assert that which was said above, namely, that a Christian is the servant of all and made subject to all. Insofar as he is free he does no works, but insofar as he is a servant he does all kinds of works. . . .

In doing these works, however, we must not think that a man is justified before God by them, for faith, which alone is righteousness before God, cannot endure that erroneous opinion. We must, however, realize that these works reduce the body to subjection and purify it of its evil lusts, and our whole purpose is to be directed only toward the driving out of lusts. Since by faith the soul is cleansed and made to love God, it desires that all things, and especially its own body, shall be purified so that all things may join with it in loving and praising God. Hence a man cannot be idle, for the need of his body drives him and he is compelled to do many good works to reduce it to subjection. Nevertheless the works themselves do not justify him before God, but he does the works out of spontaneous love in obedience to God and considers nothing except the approval of God, whom he would most scrupulously obey in all things. . . .

Let this suffice concerning works in general and at the same time concerning the works which a Christian does for himself. Lastly, we shall also speak of the things which he does toward his neighbor. A man does not live for himself alone . . . but he lives also for all men on earth; rather, he lives only for others and not for himself. To this end he brings his body into subjection that he may the more sincerely and freely serve others . . . . He cannot ever in this life be idle and without works toward his neighbors, for he will necessarily speak, deal with, and exchange views with men . . . .

Our faith in Christ does not free us from works but from false opinions concerning works, that is, from the foolish presumption that justification is acquired by works. Faith redeems, corrects, and preserves our consciences so that we know that righteousness does not consist in works, although works neither can nor ought to be wanting; just as we cannot be without food and drink and all the works of this mortal body, yet our righteousness is not in them, but in faith; and yet those works of the body are not to be despised or neglected on that account. In this world we are bound by the needs of our bodily life, but we are not righteous because of them.

Translation by W. A. Lambert, rev. Harold J. Grimm, from *Career of the Reformer: I*, ed. Harold J. Grimm, *Luther's Works,* American Edition, 31 (Philadelphia: Muhlenberg [Fortress] Press, 1957), 343 – 46, 348 – 49, 355, 358 – 59, 364 – 65, 372 – 73.

NO. 4 THE RADICAL REFORMATION

About 1560, and thus after the debacle of the Munsterite theocracy, a Dutch Anabaptist named Dietrich Philips (1504 – 68) wrote a vigorous and systematic delineation of the church as he saw it. Part II of his book, The Church of God, *deals with the seven ordinances of the true church which, according to the Anabaptist view, had been restored along apostolic lines. The many supporting references to Scripture have been deleted.*

THE SEVEN ORDINANCES OF THE TRUE CHURCH

The *first ordinance* is that the congregation above all other things must have the pure and unfalsified doctrine of the divine Word and along with it correct ministers *(Dienaers);* both are regularly called and chosen by the Lord and the congregation of the Lord. . . . The true ministers of the divine Word are easily recognized by the saving teachings of Jesus Christ, by their godly walk, and by the fruits which they bear, and moreover by the persecution which they must suffer for the sake of truth and righteousness. . . .

The *second ordinance* which Christ established in his congregation is the proper, Scriptural use of the sacraments of Jesus Christ, that is, of baptism and the Supper. For the penitent, believing and reborn children of God must be baptized and for them the Supper of the Lord pertains . . . .

The *third ordinance* is the foot washing of the saints, which Jesus Christ commanded his disciples to observe, and this for two reasons. First, he would have us know that he himself must cleanse us after the inner man, and that we must allow him to wash away the sins which beset us and all filthiness of the flesh and the spirit, that we may become purer from day to day . . . .

The second reason why Jesus instituted foot washing is that we should humble ourselves toward one another, and that we should hold our fellow believers in the highest respect, for the reason that they are the saints of God and members of the body of Jesus Christ, and that the Holy Spirit dwells in them . . . .

The *fourth ordinance* is evangelical separation, without which the congregation of God cannot stand or be maintained. For if the unfruitful branches of the vine are not pruned away they will injure the good and fruitful branches. If offending members are not cut off, the whole body must perish, that is, if open sinners, transgressors, and the disorderly are not excluded, the whole congregation must be defiled, and if false brethren are retained, we become partakers of their sins. . . .

The *fifth ordinance* is the command of love which Christ gave his disciples, saying: A new commandment I give unto you, that ye love one another, as I have loved you, that ye also love one another. By this shall all men know that ye are my disciples, if ye have love to another. From this it is easy to understand that pure brotherly love is a sure sign of genuine faith and true Christianity. . . .

From this it may be easily understood how widely those differ from the upright faith and Christianity who do not love one another, who do not prove their love toward one another by their works, but allow their poor to suffer want and openly beg for bread, against the command of the Lord, contrary to all Christian nature and contrary to brotherly love and fidelity. And, what is worse, they trespass upon, hate, envy, backbite, defame, scold, blaspheme, persecute, throttle, and kill one another, as is seen before our eyes and as their deeds amply show; and although they do this, nevertheless they want to be called Christians and the congregation of God. . . .

The *sixth ordinance* which Christ has instituted for his congregation is the keeping of all his commandments, for he demands of all his disciples a godly life, that they walk according to the gospel, openly confess the truth before men, deny self, and faithfully follow in his footsteps, voluntarily take up his cross, forsake all things, and earnestly seek first the Kingdom of God and his righteousness, the unseen heavenly things, and eternal life. He also teaches his disciples to be poor in spirit, have godly sorrow, meekness, purity of heart, mercy, peacemaking, patience in persecution for righteousness' sake, and happiness of conscience when they are despised and rejected for his name's sake . . . .

The *seventh ordinance* is that all Christians must suffer and be persecuted, as Christ has promised them and said thus: The world shall have joy, but ye shall have tribulation: but be of good cheer, for your sorrow shall be turned into joy . . . . In short, the entire Holy Scripture testifies that the righteous must suffer and possess his soul through suffering . . . .

Thus must the true Christians here be persecuted for the sake of truth and righteousness, but the Christians persecute no one on account of his faith. For Christ sends his disciples as sheep in the midst of wolves; but the sheep does not devour the wolf, but the wolf the sheep. Hence they can nevermore stand nor be counted as a congregation of the Lord who persecute others on account of their faith. . . .

Translation by George Huntston Williams, from *Spiritual and Anabaptist Writers,* ed. George Huntston Williams and Angel M. Mergal, *The Library of Christian Classics,* XXV, 240—55. Published simultaneously in Great Britain and the United States of America by SCM Press Ltd., London, and The Westminster Press, Philadelphia. First published in 1957. Used by permission.

NO. 5 JOHN CALVIN

Calvin's Institutes of the Christian Religion *contains the essentials of his theology. The selections here given show his characteristic stress on Christian self-denial and submission to God and on our utter dependence on His will for our eternal destiny.*

THE SUM OF THE CHRISTIAN LIFE: THE DENIAL OF OURSELVES

Even though the law of the Lord provides the finest and best-disposed method of ordering a man's life, it seemed good to the Heavenly Teacher to shape his people by an even more explicit plan to that rule which he had set forth in the

law. Here, then, is the beginning of this plan: the duty of
believers is "to present their bodies to God as a living sacrifice,
holy and acceptable to him," and in this consists the lawful
worship of him. From this is derived the basis of the exhortation that "they be not conformed to the fashion of this world,
but be transformed by the renewal of their minds, so that
they may prove what is the will of God." Now the great thing
is this: we are consecrated and dedicated to God in order that
we may thereafter think, speak, meditate, and do, nothing
except to his glory. . . .

We are not our own: let not our reason nor our will,
therefore, sway our plans and deeds. We are not our own:
let us therefore not set it as our goal to seek what is expedient
for us according to the flesh. We are not our own: in so far
as we can, let us therefore forget ourselves and all that
is ours. . . .

Let this therefore be the first step, that a man depart
from himself in order that he may apply the whole force
of his ability in the service of the Lord. I call "service" not
only what lies in obedience to God's Word but what turns the
mind of man, empty of its own carnal sense, wholly to the
bidding of God's Spirit. While it is the first entrance to life,
all philosophers were ignorant of this transformation, which
Paul calls "renewal of the mind." For they set up reason
alone as the ruling principle in man, and think that it alone
should be listened to; to it alone, in short, they entrust the
conduct of life. But the Christian philosophy bids reason
give way to, submit and subject itself to, the Holy Spirit so
that the man himself may no longer live but hear Christ
living and reigning within him.

From this also follows this second point: that we seek
not the things that are ours but those which are of the Lord's
will and will serve to advance his glory. This is also evidence
of great progress: that, almost forgetful of ourselves, surely
subordinating our self-concern, we try faithfully to devote
our zeal to God and his commandments. For when Scripture
bids us leave off self-concern, it not only erases from our
minds the yearning to possess, the desire for power, and
the favor of men, but it also uproots ambition and all craving
for human glory and other more secret plagues. Accordingly,

the Christian must surely be so disposed and minded that he feels within himself it is with God he has to deal throughout his life. In this way, as he will refer all he has to God's decision and judgment, so will he refer his whole intention of mind scrupulously to Him. For he who has learned to look to God in all things that he must do, at the same time avoids all vain thoughts. This, then, is that denial of self which Christ enjoins with such great earnestness upon his disciples at the outset of their service . . . .

ETERNAL ELECTION, BY WHICH GOD
HAS PREDESTINED SOME TO SALVATION,
OTHERS TO DESTRUCTION

No one who wishes to be thought religious dares simply deny predestination, by which God adopts some to hope of life, and sentences others to eternal death. But our opponents, especially those who make foreknowledge its cause, envelop it in numerous petty objections. We, indeed, place both doctrines in God, but we say that subjecting one to the other is absurd.

When we attribute foreknowledge to God, we mean that all things always were, and perpetually remain, under his eyes, so that to his knowledge there is nothing future or past, but all things are present. And they are present in such a way that he not only conceives them through ideas, as we have before us those things which our minds remember, but he truly looks upon them and discerns them as things placed before him. And this foreknowledge is extended throughout the universe to every creature. We call predestination God's eternal decree, by which he determined with himself what he willed to become of each man. For all are not created in equal condition; rather, eternal life is foreordained for some, eternal damnation for others. Therefore, as any man has been created to one or the other of these ends, we speak of him as predestined to life or to death. . . .

We assert that, with respect to the elect, this plan was founded upon his freely given mercy, without regard to human worth; but by his just and irreprehensible but incomprehensible judgment he has barred the door of life to those whom he has given over to damnation. Now among the elect we regard the call as a testimony of election. Then we hold justification another sign of its manifestation, until they come into the glory in which the fulfillment of that election lies.

From *Calvin: Institutes of the Christian Religion,* trans. Ford Lewis Battles, ed. John T. McNeill, *The Library of Christian Classics,* XX – XXI, 689 – 91, 926, 931. Published simultaneously in the United States of America and in Great Britain by The Westminster Press, Philadelphia, and SCM Press Ltd., London. Copyright © 1960 W. L. Jenkins. Used by permission.

NO. 6 CALVINISTIC ORDINANCES

In February 1547 the following Ordinances for the Supervision of Churches in the Country *were put into effect for the villages dependent on the rule of Geneva. The excerpts are indicative of the strict discipline imposed by Calvin in the attempt to enforce piety and Christian conduct.*

Sermons: Everyone in each house is to come on Sundays, unless it be necessary to leave someone behind to take care of children or animals, under penalty of 3 sous. . . . Those who have man or maid servants, are to bring them or have them conveyed when possible, so that they do not live like cattle without instruction. Everyone is to be present at Sermon when the prayer is begun, under penalty as above, unless he absent himself for legitimate reason. Everyone is to pay attention during Sermon, and there is to be no disorder or scandal. No one is to leave or go out from the church until the prayer be made at the end of Sermon, under penalty as above, unless he have legitimate cause.

Penalties: If during Sermon anyone make any disturbance or scandal, he is to be reported to the Consistory to be cautioned, in order that procedure be in proportion to the fault; that is, if by carelessness he is to be well told off, if it happen by intended malice or rebelliousness he is to be reported to their Lordships to be punished appropriately. . . .

Of Baptism: Baptism is to be administered any day,

provided that there be Sermon along with it. The Ministers are always to exhort the people to link it up with the Catechism. . . . If midwives usurp the office of Baptism, they are to be reproved or chastised according to the measure of fault found, since no commission is given them in this matter, under penalty of being put on bread and water for three days and fined ten sous; and all who consent to this action or conceal it will be liable to the same penalty.

Of the Supper: No one is to be received at the Supper unless he first have made confession of his faith. That is to say, he must declare before the Minister that he desires to live according to the reformation of the gospel, and that he knows the Creed, the Lord's Prayer and the Commandments of God. Those who wish to receive the Supper are to come at the beginning of the Service; those who come at the end are not to be received. . . .

Superstitions: Those found to have any paternosters [rosaries] or idols for adoration are to be brought before the Consistory, and, besides the punishment imposed on them there, they are to be brought before their Lordships. Those who have been on pilgrimages or voyages the same. Those who observe the papistical feasts or fastings are to be admonished only, unless they are obstinate in their rebellion. Those who have attended mass, besides admonition, are to be brought before their Lordships. In such cases, their Lordships will have the right of chastising by means of prison or otherwise, or of punishing by extraordinary fines, at their discretion. . . .

Blasphemies: Those who have blasphemed, swearing by the body or by the blood of our Lord, or suchlike, ought to do reverence for the first time; for the second a penalty of five sous; for the third ten sous; and for the last time put in the pillory for an hour. Anyone who abjures or renounces God or his Baptism is for the first time to be put for ten days on bread and water; for the second and third time he is to be punished with some more rigorous corporal punishment, at the discretion of their Lordships.

Drunkenness: There is to be no treating of one another to drinks, under penalty of three sous. The taverns are to be closed during Service, under penalty that the taverner pay three sous and anyone entering them the same. If anyone be found drunk, he is to pay for the first time three sous and be brought before the Consistory; the second time he must pay the sum of five sous; and the third [time] ten sous and be put in prison. There are to be no carousals, under penalty of ten sous.

Songs and Dances: If anyone sings songs that are unworthy, dissolute or outrageous, or spin wildly round in the dance, or the like, he is to be imprisoned for three days, and then sent on to the Consistory.

Usury: No one is to lend at interest or for profit greater than five per cent, on pain of confiscation of the capital sum and of being required to make appropriate amends according to the needs of the case.

Games: No one is to play at games that are dissolute, or at games played for gold or silver or at excessive expense, on pain of five sous and loss of the sum staked.

From *Calvin: Theological Treatises,* trans. with introductions and notes by J. K. S. Reid, *The Library of Christian Classics,* XXII, 77 − 82. Published simultaneously in Great Britain and the United States of America by SCM Press Ltd., London, and The Westminster Press, Philadelphia. First published in 1954. Used by permission.

NO. 7 THE COUNTER REFORMATION

The Catholic Counter Reformation stressed internal revivification as well as opposition to Protestantism. The Rules for Thinking with the Church, *a part of the* Spiritual Exercises *of Ignatius Loyola, indicate this leader's concern for orthodoxy and for uniformity of thinking among Roman Catholics. Loyola felt that these rules "should be explained chiefly to those who live in places or with persons whose orthodoxy is suspected; and secondly, to all workers and preachers, because they are directly opposed to the opinions and words of the heretics of our time."*

RULES FOR THINKING WITH THE CHURCH

In order to think truly, as we ought, in the Church Militant, the following rules should be observed.

The first: Laying aside all private judgment, we ought to hold our minds prepared and prompt to obey in all things the true Spouse of Christ our Lord, which is our holy Mother, the hierarchical Church.

The second: To praise confession to a priest, and the reception of the Most Holy Sacrament once a year, and much better every month, and much better still every eight days, with the requisite and due conditions.

The third: To praise the frequent hearing of Mass, also chants, psalms, and prolonged prayers both in and out of church; likewise the hours ordained at fixed times for the whole divine office, and for prayer of every kind, and all canonical Hours.

The fourth: To praise greatly Religious Orders, virginity and continency, and matrimony not so much as any of these.

The fifth: To praise vows of Religion, of obedience, of poverty, of chastity, and of other works of perfection and supererogation. . . .

The Sixth: To praise the relics of saints, paying veneration to the relics, and praying to the saints; and to praise likewise stations, pilgrimages, indulgences, jubilees, cruzadas, and candles lighted in churches.

The seventh: To praise the enactments of the Church with regard to fasts and abstinences, as those of Lent, Ember days, Vigils, Fridays, and Saturdays; likewise penances, not only interior but also exterior.

The eighth: To praise the building and adornment of churches; and also images, and to venerate them according to what they represent.

The ninth: To praise in fine all the precepts of the Church, preserving a ready mind to seek reasons for defending her, and in no way impugning her.

The tenth: We ought to be more ready to approve and praise the enactments and recommendation, and also the customs of our superiors; because, although sometimes they may not be or may not have been praise-worthy, still to speak against them, whether in public discourse or before the common people, would give rise to murmurs and scandal, rather than edification; and thus the people would be irritated against their superiors, whether temporal or spiritual. . . .

The eleventh: To praise theology, positive and scholastic. . . .

The twelfth: We ought to guard against making comparisons between ourselves who are now living and the blessed who have passed away, for no slight error is committed in this. . . .

The thirteenth: To arrive at the truth in all things, we ought always to be ready to believe that what seems to us white is black, if the hierarchical Church so defines it. . . .

The fourteenth: Although it is very true that no one can be saved unless he is predestined, and has faith and grace, we must be very careful in our manner of speaking and treating of these subjects.

The fifteenth: We ought not habitually to speak much of predestination; but if sometimes mention should be made of it in any way, we must so speak that the common people may not fall into any error. . . . and therewith becoming paralyzed they neglect good works conducive to their salvation, and to the spiritual profit of their souls.

The sixteenth: In the same way we must take heed lest by speaking much and with great earnestness on faith, without any distinction and explanation, occasion be given to become slothful and negligent in good works, whether before faith is formed by charity or after.

The seventeenth: In like manner we ought not to speak of grace at such length and so vehemently as to give rise to that poisonous teaching which takes away free-will. . . .

The eighteenth: Although it is above all things praiseworthy to serve God our Lord diligently out of pure love, yet we ought greatly to praise the fear of His divine Majesty; because not only is filial fear a pious and most holy thing, but even servile fear. . . .

The Spiritual Exercises of Saint Ignatius of Loyola, trans. W. H. Longridge (London: Roxburghe House, 1919), pp. 197–200.

SUGGESTIONS FOR FURTHER READING

Few periods in history have been studied and described as much as the three important centuries between 1300 and 1600. Innumerable paperback studies on the various aspects, institutions, movements, and personages of the Renaissance and Reformation periods are available. Only a few important works are listed here.

Useful reference works containing many informative articles are *The Catholic Encyclopedia,* 16 vols. (New York, 1907 – 12); *The New Schaff-Herzog Encyclopedia of Religious Knowledge,* 12 vols. (New York, 1908 – 12); and *The Oxford Dictionary of the Christian Church* (London, 1957). *The Cambridge Medieval History,* Vols. VI – VIII (Cambridge, 1924 – 36), and *The New Cambridge Modern History,* Vols. I and II (Cambridge, 1957 – 58), include important general studies.

A 56-volume set of the writings of Luther in English is now being published as a joint venture of Concordia Publishing House (St. Louis) and Fortress Press (Philadelphia). Informative, highly readable, and well-illustrated accounts of Luther's life are those of Ernest G. Schwiebert, *Luther and His Times: The Reformation from a New Perspective* (St. Louis: Concordia Publishing House, 1950), and Roland H. Bainton, *Here I Stand: A Life of Martin Luther* (New York, Nashville: Abingdon-Cokesbury Press, 1950). A more recent biography with many illustrations and quotations is by M. A. Kleeberg and Gerhard Lemme, *In the Footsteps of Martin Luther,* trans. Erich Hopka (St. Louis: Concordia Publishing House, 1966). A good general study of another reformer and his church is *The History and Character of Calvinism,* by John T. McNeill (New York: Oxford University Press, 1954; paperback ed., Galaxy Book 190, 1967).

Valuable source readings for the period can be found in Vols. XIII to XXVI of *The Library of Christian Classics,* ed. John Baillie et al. (Philadelphia: Westminster Press). These volumes contain important works from the late medieval mystics and from Wycliffe, Erasmus, Luther (4 vols.), Melanchthon, Bucer, Calvin (4 vols.), Zwingli, Bullinger, spiritual and Anabaptist writers, and the English Reformation.

Many brief documents of the Reformation period are assembled in Hans J. Hillerbrand's *The Reformation: A Narrative History Related by Contemporary Observers and Participants* (New York and Evanston: Harper & Row, 1964). Contemporary illustrations and informative texts can be found in the *Illustrated History of the Reformation,* ed. Oskar Thulin (Saint Louis: Concordia Publishing House, 1967) and *The Reformation,* ed. Edith Simon and the editors of Time-Life Books (New York: Time Inc., 1966).

Index